CHELTENHAM'S TRAMS & EARLY BUSES

One of the later tramcars in the fleet of the Cheltenham & District Light Railway Co was no.23, seen here at the St Mark's depot when newly delivered in 1921. It was one of four ordered from English Electric but, in the event, only three were delivered to the Cheltenham system. They were the first new cars for Cheltenham since 1905, and enabled some of the earlier cars to be withdrawn from service. Unlike earlier cars they were able to operate on the Cleeve Hill service without any modifications to their brakes. As can be seen in this view, these cars had conventional left-ascending staircases as opposed to the reversed stairs fitted to all earlier Cheltenham cars. The name of Mr H.J. McCormick, the General Manager, may be seen neatly signwritten beneath the word 'Railway'. Its sister car, no.21, was rescued for preservation and remains in Cheltenham today. (Gloucestershire Echo)

CHELTENHAM'S TRAMS & EARLY BUSES

Colin Martin

TEMPUS

First published 2001
Copyright © Colin Martin, 2001

Tempus Publishing Limited
The Mill, Brimscombe Port,
Stroud, Gloucestershire, GL5 2QG
www.tempus-publishing.com

ISBN 0 7524 2121 2

Typesetting and origination by
Tempus Publishing Limited
Printed in Great Britain by
Midway Colour Print, Wiltshire

The 1934 Weymann-bodied petrol-engined AEC Regents were handsome vehicles, very different from the town's first double-deckers delivered less than five years earlier. With Cheltenham College in the background, nos 2 and 4 (DG 9819/21) pass each other as they operate Service 3 between Leckhampton and the town centre. The AECs had displaced open-top Guys from this route, with these in turn freeing up some single-deckers for disposal. The photograph was taken soon after the vehicles had been delivered; both had already attracted advertising for local companies (Locke's the bakers, Regent Motors and Collins Bros, manufacturers of pies and sausages). (Author's collection)

Contents

Acknowledgements

My researches for this volume have caused me to dig deeply and frequently into material held in the reference department of Cheltenham's Public Library, and in particular into the minutes of Cheltenham Town Council and its sub-committees, the *Gloucestershire Echo* and the *Cheltenham Chronicle*. The *Cheltenham Looker-On* has also filled in some gaps in my knowledge. I am grateful both to the Gloucestershire County Council's staff at the Library for their assistance, and to the Editor of the *Gloucestershire Echo* for allowing me to extract items from issues of long ago. Rather more specialist information has come from the Tramway Museum Society, the PSV Circle and the Gloucestershire Records Office, to the members and staff of which my thanks are also extended.

Many of the photographs are the results of the efforts of a team of early transport enthusiasts in the town; from the 1920s the late Leslie Lapper, Graham Lloyd, Noel Meanwell and Norman Willis made a determined effort to capture the town's trams and buses on film. To fill in gaps in their own coverage, they acquired photographs from any other available source. Their endeavours produced several exceptionally comprehensive albums depicting the development of the town's public transport through the first seventy years of the twentieth century. I have drawn upon these albums, not only for the photographs themselves, but also for the information which the prints reveal; where photographs are not individually acknowledged it may be assumed that they came either from this pooled resource, or from my own collection. Particular thanks are due to Mr and Mrs Hoare, as custodians of the Lapper collection, for their patient assistance. Once again the *Gloucestershire Echo* and its erstwhile weekly sister paper, the *Cheltenham Chronicle* were most useful sources of photographs. Frank Wood and Len Edwards, both of whom spent all of their working lives on the town's buses (and trams in the former case) have also shared their memories and provided photographs and information. Photographs were also generously made available by the following: Cheltenham Art Gallery and Museum, Peter Davey of Bristol, Roy Marshall of Burnley, Phil Moth (PM Transport Photography) of Camberley, The Omnibus Society, David Packer of Bromley and Mike Rooum of Coleford and the late F. Baldwin. The copyright of those attributed to the late W.J. Haynes is now held by the author.

The original source of a handful of photographs is not entirely clear; while every effort has been made to obtain permission from appropriate copyright holders, I regret that in a very small number of cases these could not be identified or located.

I am also grateful for the assistance given by Geoff Bruce of Bristol, John Gillham of Ealing, Alan Oxley of Attenborough and Graham Teasdill of Bournemouth.

And finally my thanks to David Lyall who read the drafts of the tramway chapters in considerable detail and drew my attention to a number of areas needing further work; should any errors remain they are of course fully my responsibility.

Colin Martin
Woodmancote, March 2001

Introduction

The evolution of urban transport in Cheltenham has followed a course similar in many respects to that to be found in many other provincial towns. However, as will become clear from a number of the events documented within this volume, its progress in this spa town was at some stages rather more erratic than might reasonably have been expected. As successive proposals for perceived improvements in the town's transport systems were placed before its members, the Town Council often found itself in a dilemma. It had the unenviable task of striking an appropriate balance between providing Cheltonians with improved facilities, and ensuring that the important and unique qualities of the Gloucestershire spa town would not be adversely affected by such changes.

In this first volume, the history of the town's public transport is traced from the introduction of regular horse bus services in 1890, through the tramway era to the end of the first full decade of motor bus operation. It is all too easy to try to visualise those late nineteenth century operations against the background of the town as we know it today. We need to remember that motor vehicles had not appeared on the scene, that roads were unmetalled and that the horse reigned supreme for both local and long distance road journeys. By contrast, the rail network was well established throughout the land with Cheltenham already served by several important lines. Providing local services to the town's main railway station was therefore an important objective for the initial horse bus service; somewhat curiously however, the early rounds of discussion concerning the optimum route for the tramway took neither of the main railway stations into account.

Cheltenham was narrowly denied the opportunity to experience the benefits of a horse-drawn tramway system, but this only led to its residents being all the more ready for the electric tramway when it was constructed in stages during the first five years of the twentieth century. During that period, the horse bus services disappeared in a somewhat unsympathetic manner, which for several years left residents in parts of the town without the transport to which they had become accustomed. The trams were to serve the town well for thirty years; regular motor bus services commenced to other areas of the town in 1924, before additional buses progressively replaced the trams during 1930.

Unlike that of many towns, Cheltenham's transport system was never in the ownership of the municipality, the services have always been provided by commercial organisations. This is by no means due to any closed minds on the part of the council: the ownership of the undertaking has been the subject of frequent debate over many years, producing many lively exchanges within the council chamber.

1939 proved to be a convenient time to end the first volume of this historical review. By then the town had expanded steadily to boundaries with which many readers will still be able to identify. Bus design had developed rapidly and so successfully that even the older vehicles still at work in the town in the early 1970s continued to reflect the same basic design principles. 1939 was also significant as being the year in which one of the major changes in the ownership of the town's bus service provider was to occur. Finally, the onset of the Second World War in that same year was to have a major impact on the requirement for transport, and the availability of both vehicles and staff.

2001 is the centenary of the introduction of tramway services in the town. This has proved a sufficient catalyst for me to complete this work which had been a gleam in my eye for many years.

A companion volume continues the story of the town's buses: *Cheltenham's Buses 1939 - 1980*.

A two-horse bus passes Pittville Gates as it makes its way from the direction of Prestbury towards the town centre. Horse bus services were introduced on this route in 1890; they initially terminated at Pittville, later continued to Prestbury and finally reached Southam. On the board displayed to the right of the driver the route within the town is summarised as 'Pittville, Montpellier and Lansdown'. The top deck passengers are using parasols to protect themselves from the summer sunshine. The union flags, bunting and the photographs of the Queen Victoria and the late Prince Albert displayed on the terraced buildings suggest that the year was 1897, the Queen's Diamond Jubilee.

One

Horse-Buses Appear on the Streets

While there is no doubt that the earliest public transport in Cheltenham was horse-drawn, there is some room for debate as to when it first appeared. An 1879 edition of the *Gloucestershire Echo* makes passing reference to the appearance in the town some twenty-five years earlier of a horse bus service; the report indicates that this facility was quickly withdrawn 'as nobody used it and the whole thing was a failure'. As the report is based only upon the rather generalised recollections of a town councillor, no firm date can be attached to this development. However, as it was apparently a short-lived venture, it may be assumed not to have had any significant impact on the lives of the local community.

It was some thirty-five years after that first ill-fated venture that Cheltonians were provided once more with horse bus services. This time the business was to prove rather more enduring. Over the ensuing century the services it introduced were to metamorphose firstly into a network of tramway routes, and eventually into the motor bus network we can see at work in the town today.

In September 1889 a group of Birmingham businessmen let it be known that they were prepared to invest half of the capital required to establish 'cheap and regular locomotion' to meet what they considered to be a long-needed requirement of the residents of the spa town. The *Cheltenham Looker-On* expressed doubts that such a requirement did indeed exist. It pointed out that the two principal hotels sent their own 'omnibuses' to meet every train at the town's two main railway stations, while the general public were faced with a superfluity of cabs and pony carriages running over every thoroughfare in the town. The report went on to suggest that the appearance of a number of 'Birmingham Omnibuses' in the town would only disrupt the flow of traffic in the High Street and do little to enhance the overall quality of life in the town.

On the twenty-first of that month, the promoters of the horse bus scheme called a meeting at the Cheltenham Corn Exchange with the aim of securing the support of the town's business community. The intention was declared of operating half a dozen omnibuses, running from the centre at a frequency of fifteen minutes to various areas of the town. The meeting ended with a decision that a committee would be established to draw up a formal prospectus. That prospectus was published the following spring and is reproduced in full on page 13. It may be noted that the cars were to be 'one-man operated'. The routes envisaged would connect Lansdown Castle and the Midland Railway Station with Pittville Gates, Leckhampton with the Tewkesbury Road Gas Works, Charlton Kings with the Great Western Railway Station (St James') and Prestbury with the town centre. Valuable additional revenue would be generated by the display of advertisements on the sides of the cars.

The business was eventually incorporated on 9 April 1890 under the name of the Cheltenham Omnibus Co. and its seven directors all quoted addresses in the town. The prospectus offered 5,000 £1 shares. The response from the public was much slower than anticipated and it proved necessary for the list of subscribers to be kept open until 24 May that year, a full month later than had been envisaged. However, services were able to commence operation between the Midland Station and Pittville Gates on 2 June 1890 and later that month the service to Charlton Kings was introduced.

A meeting of shareholders on 6 August 1890 reported that the company had acquired stabling at 4 Regent Street, in the town centre, and that 3,000 shares had been taken up. Fifteen horses were now in use and three buses had been purchased; this figure included the 'large yellow bus' but excluded the 'experimental red bus' which was then on loan. Two more small buses were on order and early delivery was expected. Two brakes and a wagonette had also been purchased. The yellow bus was reported to have ousted the small red vehicle from the Lansdown-Pittville service, the latter bus now being deployed on the High Street - Charlton Kings route. When the other two buses arrived, one would be used to introduce the service to Leckhampton, while the second would be an additional vehicle on the Pittville - Lansdown route, doubling the frequency to every thirty minutes.

The company was reported to have ten employees, and to have carried 15,000 passengers in its first two months of operations. The new small buses would not have any outside seats, as vehicles so equipped required two horses. They would be able to seat ten inside, with a further four alongside the driver.

The directors made an appeal to passengers to alight at street corners rather than outside their own houses in order to reduce the number of times the horses had to pull away, such effort making them tire much more quickly. The meeting was also informed that fare evasion was already a problem, particularly with passengers paying the minimum fare of 1d and travelling much further than such a fare entitled them. The service to Leckhampton duly commenced operation on 1 November 1890.

At the company's first Annual General Meeting the following March it was recorded that the lease on office premises in Royal Crescent Mews had been acquired and that services were initially operated using horses hired from Birmingham, proving very expensive. By 31 December 1890, twenty-nine horses had been acquired and the fleet consisted of four two-horse 'large' omnibuses and two one-horse 'small' buses. Takings in the first seven months stood at £879 0s 4d. While this was declared to be satisfactory, it was clearly somewhat disappointing. A period of bad weather was blamed for the operation running at a loss for some weeks during the winter months, but the meeting heard that since February the company had been consistently making a profit. There were now plans for the service, already extended from Pittville to Prestbury, to run on further to serve Southam. The directors prided themselves on the buses 'being an ornament as well as of use to the town'. A query as to why the earlier intention of having a dozen vehicles in service by this time had not materialised brought a rather spurious explanation from one of the quick-thinking directors. He suggested that on the basis that each of the two-horse buses actually equated to two of the originally intended vehicles, the fleet effectively now had the equivalent of ten vehicles – more or less as planned!

The main discussion at the March 1892 Annual General Meeting concerned the operation of Sunday services, which had recently been withdrawn. A ballot of shareholders revealed that 332 were in favour of their being resumed, with only 105 against. Receipts for the year stood at £3,372 7s 1d, to give a positive balance of £435 10s. Five two-horse buses and two one-horse buses were in operation and a further two-horse bus was on order. Thirty-nine horses were owned. Despite the encouraging number of passengers, almost all continued to purchase 1d tickets. It was agreed that the financial situation would not permit the operation of evening buses from the town centre.

One year later the news was not good. The balance sheet showed a profit of £117 but this was insufficient to balance depreciation. Receipts had increased, but not by as much as expenditure. Traffic was good in summer, but poor in winter. This confirmed the long-held view that the service was used essentially for pleasure and social recreational purposes rather than for regular 'commuting'. The best day of the year for takings was Whit Monday, when receipts reached £120. Twelve horses had been sold, and three had died – none had been replaced.

The situation was even worse the following year. At the 1894 Annual General Meeting a diminution of receipts was reported, leading to a deficiency on the balance sheets. In mitigation it was pointed out that the prices of hay and straw were adversely affecting the profitability of bus operators across the whole country. To make matters worse, takings were down a little at £3,044. To compensate for the increasing imbalance between takings and costs, the number of journeys had been cut back in 1893. It was also recognised that too many buses had previously been owned; this had now been remedied. Before the reduction had been made, at the end of 1893, the fleet consisted of six large and five small buses, along with one (horse-drawn) charabanc. One small brake had been sold and another had been traded in for the charabanc. The stables currently housed thirty-two horses.

Operationally, the Pittville service was now consistently commencing its journeys from St Mark's; apparently for some time it had been cut back to the Ladies College, presumably from their premises in Bayshill Road. 'St Mark's' is probably a reference in this case to the area usually referred to as Lansdown Castle. This route was running every thirty minutes to Pittville but with alternate vehicles working through to Southam. Loadings on the Leckhampton and Charlton Kings routes were such that large vehicles were needed during the summer months to maintain the basic hourly frequency but in the afternoons a small bus was also put out on each route to give a thirty minute headway. The cost of each horse was calculated to be 15s 10d per week.

No further references have been found to the state of the company's affairs, but despite its precarious financial situation, it clearly managed to pull through. The minutes of the Cheltenham Corporation's General Purposes and Watch Committee indicate that the fleet continued to undergo change. In May 1896 for example the committee approved the transfer of licence no.87 from a recently sold horse bus to a new charabanc. In 1900 an application was lodged for a further charabanc which, had it been approved, would have replaced the bus operating on licence no.1.

The two-horse buses came in two sizes. One was a little longer and immediately identifiable by the four windows on each side of its lower saloon, where the smaller vehicles had three. The open upper decks on all vehicles were accessed by curving rear staircases. The longer vehicles had forward facing seats on their upper decks, while the shorter buses had outward facing 'knife-board' seats mounted along the centre of their open decks. The buses and horses were housed at the company's stables in Regent Street. No details have been ascertained of the 'small' one-horse buses, but it is clear from the brief details given at the 1890 meeting (referred to above) that they had no upper deck as such.

Destinations were displayed on boards running the full length of the vehicles and displayed beneath the side windows. Each vehicle displayed its 'fleet' number at the lower front corner of the main side panel. In view of the wide range of these numbers, they were more likely to have been the Hackney Carriage licence numbers as allocated by the Cheltenham Corporation. Two of the four-window buses are, for example, known to have been numbered 6 and 49.

The charabancs are believed to have been used only for private party outings and are assumed to have taken the form of open brakes.

To the disgust of local cab proprietors, who lost much of their regular income through the introduction of the horse bus services, the buses proved popular with the public. Fare evasion however continued to be a problem. By 1899 a travelling inspector had to be employed to deal with those who managed to board without a ticket, or who travelled further than entitled by the fare they tendered. Yet just as the cabs had been eclipsed by the horse buses, the horse buses themselves were marginalised once the electric tramway era arrived. Services to Cleeve Hill, Southam and Prestbury were discontinued at about the time that the trams first reached those communities, in 1901. However, the western end of that service between the Midland Station and the town centre continued in operation as it offered an alternative route to the tramway by running along Queen's Road and through Montpellier and Bayshill. Somewhat surprisingly, in view of both the horse bus and tramway services between the Midland Station and the town centre, Mrs E. Martin of the Midland Temperance Hotel applied in October 1901 for a licence for a horse bus service between the Midland Station and Pittville Gates. Her application was rejected by the Town Council.

All horse bus services were withdrawn on 31 October 1902, following an agreement with the tramway operators as is explained in some detail in Chapter 4. At its close the Cheltenham Omnibus Co. claimed the following assets: 33 horses; 5 omnibuses; 3 charabancs; harness and other necessary affects and appliances. In addition, the goodwill of all contracts and agreements for advertisements on the vehicles, were estimated to bring in up to £60 per annum.

An Extraordinary General Meeting of the Cheltenham Omnibus Co. was held on 16 February 1903; this meeting passed a special resolution that the company be wound up voluntarily. Col. Richard Rogers, a one-time mayor of Cheltenham and a dentist by profession, and Mr F.H. Neale were appointed as liquidators to conduct the winding-up.

Whilst the horse bus era was relatively short-lived, it represented a significant development in the introduction of public transport to the Gloucestershire town. Until the buses appeared, the majority of the townsfolk would have been unable to afford to use any transport whatsoever. The penny fares of the buses would still have been out of reach of many, but nevertheless enabled more to travel on a regular basis, thus opening up employment opportunities, leading in turn to greater prosperity and a gradual expansion of the town itself.

One of the two-horse buses delivered to the Cheltenham Omnibus Co in the 1890s. The immaculate condition of the vehicle suggests that it had not been delivered to the company when the photograph was taken – indeed the street sign 'Black Friars' visible in the background indicates that this cannot have been in Cheltenham. The rather fragile curving rear staircase can be clearly seen, along with one of the wooden slatted seats on the upper deck. Note the clearly defined route: Ladies' College, Prestbury and Southam. Not only is this displayed on the board mounted beneath the side windows, but it is also signwritten directly onto the rear of the vehicle, a practice today referred to as 'route branding', indicating that the intention was for this vehicle to be permanently allocated to that route. Indications are that this vehicle was delivered c.1893. In 1891 it had been announced that the route to Prestbury would be extended to Southam, while in 1894 it was announced that the Ladies College service would routinely continue to St Mark's.

THE CHELTENHAM OMNIBUS COMPANY
LIMITED.

Incorporated under the Companies' Acts, 1862 to 1886, whereby the liability of the Shareholders is limited to the amount of their Shares.

CAPITAL £5,000, divided into 5,000 Shares of £1 each.

(Payable 5s. on Application; 5s. on Allotment; and the Balance as required by Instalments not exceeding 5s. per Share.)

Directors :

MAJOR-GENERAL H. B. BABBAGE (Chairman), Mayfield, Cheltenham.
LIEUT.-COLONEL F. J. ASHBURNER, 5, Lansdown Place, Cheltenham.
MR. JOHN COCKRELL, Colonnade, Cheltenham.
ALLAN ADAIR DIGHTON, Esq., Berkeley Lawn, Cheltenham.
MR. RICHARD EDE MARSHALL (Messrs. R. E. & C. MARSHALL), Clarence Street, Cheltenham.
MR. F. H. NEALE (Messrs. NEALE & SONS), Promenade Villas, Cheltenham.
LIEUT.-COLONEL RICHARD ROGERS, Fern-clyffe, Cheltenham.

Bankers :—COUNTY OF GLOUCESTER BANK, LIMITED, Cheltenham.

Solicitor:—F. PROBYN DIGHTON, Regent Street, Cheltenham.

Auditors:—MESSRS. MARRIS & DAVIES, 37, Waterloo Street, Birmingham.

Secretary *(pro tem):*—F. PROBYN DIGHTON, Cheltenham.

Veterinary Surgeons:—MESSRS. TAYLOR & HUBAND.

Registered Office :—4, REGENT STREET, CHELTENHAM.

PROSPECTUS.

THE COMPANY is formed for the purpose of running a frequent service of well-appointed Omnibuses at cheap fares from the Suburbs of Cheltenham into the Centre of the Town. This will be supplying a want long needed, as at the present time the only means of passenger transit is by hiring a cab, and this is on the some of the Routes proposed to be covered, not always possible, besides being expensive.

It will be seen by an "Estimated Trading Account," which has been very carefully prepared by practical men, that if each Omnibus only earns the average amount of 1s. per journey, a large profit will be made. The Statistics from which the items in the aforementioned account have been based were taken from several large Public Companies and Private Job Masters in London, Liverpool, and Birmingham.

The Omnibuses proposed to be used are of the newest style, and as used in London and other large towns with great success. They do not require a Conductor, thereby saving the expense of a man per vehicle. They have also been proved very safe, for the door being under the control of the driver passengers cannot get in or alight unless the Omnibus is stationary.

The proposed Routes are from "Lansdown Castle," St. Mark's, *viâ* Midland Railway Station, to Pittville Gates; Leckhampton to Gas Works; Charlton Kings to Great Western Railway Station; and from Prestbury to centre of the town; or as may be found advisable hereafter.

It is proposed to arrange the Fares as far as possible in Penny Stages, for instance, from "Lansdown Castle" to Montpellier, 1d.; from Montpellier to High Street, 1d.; from High Street to Pittville Gates, 1d.

The opening of the new Midland and South Western line, in June next, will greatly increase the traffic on the Lansdown Route, and will doubtless add considerably to the receipts of the Company.

It is also thought that a great addition can be made to the profits of the Company by running Open Breaks, or Char-a-bancs, to the various places of interest during the Summer months, a want long felt by the many visitors to our town, and will no doubt bring many more to it who are now deterred from visiting it on account of there being no cheap means of seeing the beautiful scenery surrounding us.

By allowing neat and well got up Advertisements to be exhibited on the Omnibuses the Directors hope to realize a considerable income.

Companies very similar to this have been formed in several provincial towns, and pay a good dividend, such as the Bath Road Car and Tramways Company, the Bristol Tramways and Carriage Company, and the Hastings Omnibus Company, and others.

The following Contract entered into by or on behalf of the Company may be seen at the Registered Office :

An Agreement dated the 10th day of April, 1890, and made between WILLIAM COLBURN VERITY, of 191, High Street, Cheltenham, in the County of Gloucester, Jeweller, thereinafter called the Promoter, of the one part, and ROBERT COSSENS, of 4, Regent Street, Cheltenham aforesaid, Clerk, as Trustee, on behalf of the Company, of the other part.

The Directors have been offered suitable premises for Offices, Stabling, and Stores, in a central position.

Applications for Shares should, with a remittance for the amount of the Deposit, be forwarded to or left with the Company's Bankers.

If no Allotment be made the Deposit will be returned in full, and if a smaller number of Shares be allotted than that applied for. the balance will be applied towards the amount due on Allotment.

Prospectuses may be obtained from the Bankers, Solicitor, and Offices of the Company.

The Subscription List for Shares will be open on MONDAY NEXT, the 21st day of April, and will close on SATURDAY NEXT, the 26th day of April, 1890.

APRIL, 1890.

The Prospectus of the Cheltenham Omnibus Co., as published in April 1890.

The Malvern Inn was a well-known landmark in Leckhampton Road at the point where Charlton Lane and Church Road join that main thoroughfare. The licensee at the time of this photograph was Letitia M. Kirkham. Seen outside the Inn is the two-horse bus allocated hackney licence number 6. The route of the bus is clearly shown on the slip board beneath its side windows: 'Gt Western Station, High Street, Leckhampton'. This is one of the slightly longer vehicles, with four windows and forward facing seats on the open deck. Although the buses had for some years been operated only by the driver, in this case the younger man standing with the horses was clearly acting as a conductor. This possibly indicates that the photograph was taken late on in horse bus days, c.1900.

Dating from about the same time as the view above, but this time at Six Ways on the Charlton Kings route, a very similar bus has arrived from the town centre. The driver is well wrapped up, although the trees indicate that the photograph must have been taken during the summer months. Once again there is a conductor at hand – possibly the same gentleman as above.

"THE COMPANIES ACTS, 1862 to 1900."

COMPANY LIMITED BY SHARES.

(COPY)

Special Resolution

(Pursuant to The Companies Act, 1862, Sections 50, 51, and 129)

OF THE

Cheltenham Omnibus Company, Limited.

Passed 16th February, 1903.   *Confirmed 3rd March, 1903.*

At an Extraordinary General Meeting of the Members of the above-named Company, duly convened, and held at the Company's Office, Regent Street, Cheltenham, in the County of Gloucester, on the 16th day of February, 1903, the following SPECIAL RESOLUTION was duly passed; and at a subsequent Extraordinary General Meeting of the Members of the said Company, also duly convened, and held at the same place on the 3rd day of March, 1903, the following SPECIAL RESOLUTION was duly confirmed :—

> "That the Company be wound up voluntarily, and that Colonel R. Rogers and Mr. F. H. Neale be the Liquidators to conduct the winding up."

RICHARD ROGERS.

Chairman.

Witness to the Signature of Richard Rogers—

W. G. GURNEY,

Solicitor,

CHELTENHAM.

Filed with the Registrar of Joint Stock Companies
on the 9th day of March, 1903.

JORDAN & SONS, LIMITED,
COMPANY REGISTRATION AGENTS, PRINTERS, PUBLISHERS, AND STATIONERS,
116 AND 120 CHANCERY LANE, LONDON, W.C.

A copy of the Special Resolution for the winding up of the Cheltenham Omnibus Co. – the end of a short, but nevertheless important, era in the history of Cheltenham's public transport.

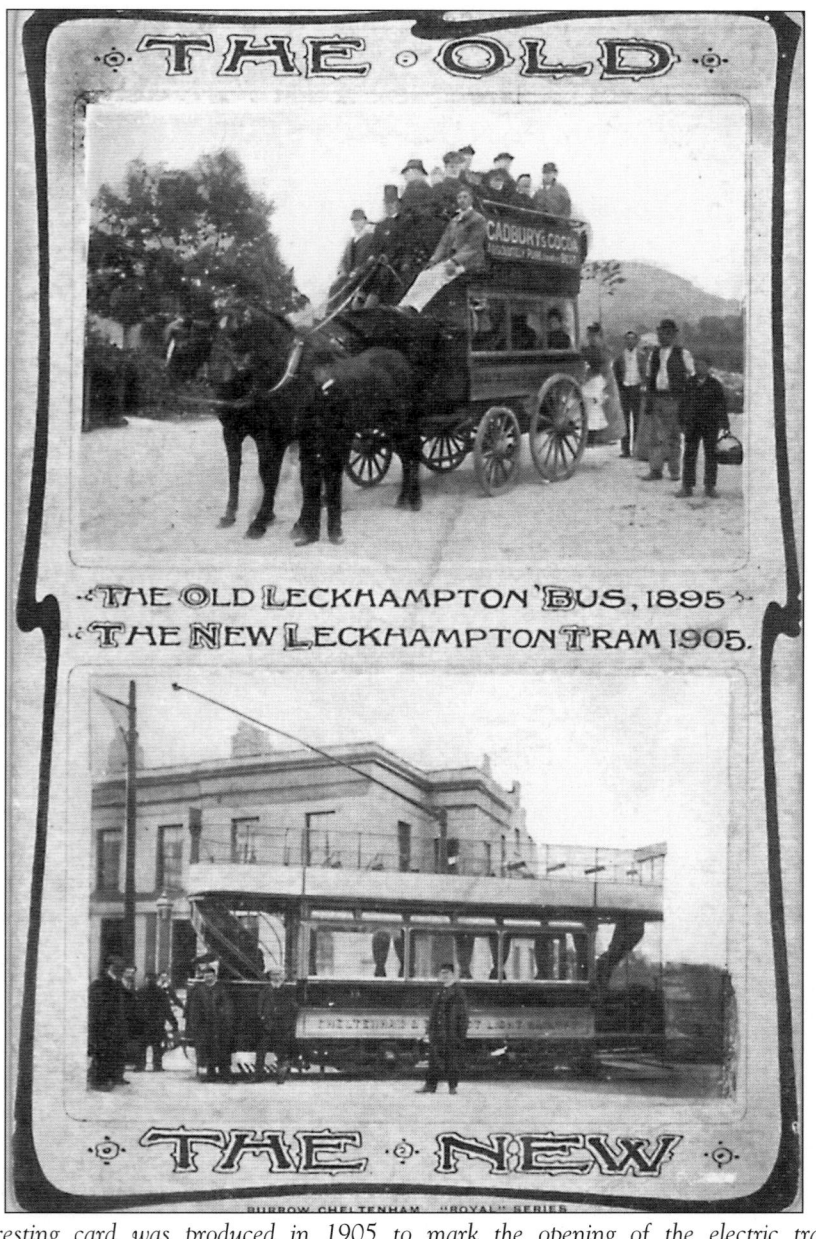

This interesting card was produced in 1905 to mark the opening of the electric tramway to Leckhampton. The upper part of the card captures one of the smaller two-horse buses, with only three windows in each side of its lower saloon and centrally-mounted outward facing seats upstairs. The bus was photographed at Leckhampton, allegedly in 1895, although an earlier date seems more likely. It appears to have been attracting much custom and interest as it awaited departure. This trip to town would have been relatively easy for the horses as there is a favourable but gentle gradient for just about the whole journey. In the lower view tramcar no.13 is seen outside the Midland Hotel. The hotel stood at the point where the line to the tram depot at St Mark's branched off from the original tram route along Gloucester Road. This was one of eight cars delivered in 1905 to operate the new services to both Leckhampton and Charlton Kings.

Two

Tramway Proposals

Previous accounts of the early negotiations over the provision of a tramway in Cheltenham have begun the story in the late 1890s, whereas Cheltenham Town Council had in fact first considered a proposal from the Street Tramway Co. twenty years earlier. It may have been coincidental, but construction of a three-mile stretch of street tramway in Gloucester, just nine miles distant, was at that time nearing completion by the Imperial Tramways Co. As some of the construction manpower and materials might still have been available in the area, there may have been a plan for local redeployment of these resources. As with most other systems of the time, including that in Gloucester, the service in Cheltenham would have been provided by four-wheel horse-drawn cars.

The Tramways Co., as promoters of the proposed Cheltenham Tramways Bill, sought the consent of the council to a scheme that would involve the construction of three lines radiating from the town centre. In December 1878, company representatives outlined their plans at a meeting with members of the town's Streets and Highways Committee. The committee's chairman brought the matter to the attention of the full council later that month. The council recognised that this was one of the most important matters to have come before them for some time. They adjourned for further consideration, much to the frustration of the promoters who had anticipated a rapid and enthusiastic response.

In the hope of hastening the council's deliberations, an open letter dated 2 January 1879 was sent to 'The Mayor, Aldermen and Burgesses of the town', by the solicitors for the Bill. It acknowledged the sensitivity of the town's Promenade and offered to re-route the proposed line away from that elegant and fashionable thoroughfare; it could instead run via Montpellier Street, Old Well Lane, Clarence Parade and Clarence Street. The letter indicated that lines would be constructed to a gauge of 3ft 6in and confirmed that the service would use only 'light one-horse cars'. The letter went on to offer an extension of one line to Leckhampton railway station; it is however not otherwise clear as to exactly where the three lines of which the promoters spoke were to run.

The town's Streets and Highways Committee considered the proposal during January 1879 and voted in favour of recommending assent to the full council. After a four-hour meeting on 3 February 1879, the Town Council voted against the scheme by eleven votes to ten. The promoters responded by seeking approval for the installation of a short length of track for a two-week period in order that a demonstration might be made of a single tramcar between the municipal offices (then in the High Street) and the Fleece Hotel. At their meeting of 1 March 1879, the council agreed that this demonstration might proceed, but with the track to be laid in another part of the High Street. The promoters' cause was not helped by a letter which appeared in the *Cheltenham Chronicle* from a gentleman living in Gloucester, who congratulated the council on the wisdom of their move to withhold support on the basis of the situation in his own city. There the streets had been in turmoil during the construction of the tramway, completion of which had resulted in the useable width of the road for other purposes having been reduced to virtually nothing!

In the hope of getting the support of the wider public, the promoters called a meeting in the town on 2 April. They subsequently claimed that all 1,200 persons present had supported the motion that 'this meeting respectfully urges the Town Council to give the requisite assent to the Cheltenham Tramways Bill'. When the council considered the issue a few days later, they again voted, still by a majority of only one, not to give the necessary support. The trial track was presumably never laid. *The Cheltenham Chronicle* of 8 April 1879 reported as follows:

> *The majority of our readers will be pleased to learn that our Town Council have for the second time by a majority of one refused their assent to the application to lay down tramways in our beautiful town. We trust we have heard the last of them and that the company of speculative gentlemen will seek 'fresh scenes and pastures new' to find investment opportunities for their surplus capital. A more unsuitable place for the introduction of tramways than the fashionable town of Cheltenham does not exist.*

These few lines of the *Chronicle* report will help to set the scene for the cautious mood of the town towards any form of development which might threaten its Regency grandeur and tranquillity. Cheltenham purported to enjoy a certain exclusivity following the patronage of George III towards the end of the previous century. Promoters of later schemes were to find that they would need to tread very carefully when presenting their proposals to the town. As subsequent chapters will reveal, such developments were eventually permitted. They were to provide the good folk of Cheltenham with a succession of transport systems capable of meeting the needs of all classes, the distinction between which was still very marked in some of the early tramways debates. Frequent references were made to three main groups of residents: retired officers, businessmen and artisans!

Following the rejection of the 1879 proposals, all went quiet on the tramway front for no less than seventeen years. This should perhaps have come as no surprise. Although the strength of the council's opposition was not quite as great as the euphoria of the *Chronicle's* comments might have suggested, potential promoters would understandably have been wary about risking both their reputations and the initial survey costs on a similar refusal from Cheltenham, when there were many other towns still without a tramway system. Besides, the town was physically compact and those living on its outer fringes were, in the main, wealthy for their time. In many cases, they would have owned their own carriages, or would have had the means to travel regularly by one of the horse-drawn cabs with which the town was adequately equipped. Those who could not afford to travel probably had little need so to do; the town centre was encircled by areas of compact terraced housing, all within easy reach of most places of employment. But things had begun to change in the 1890s, as we have already seen, with the creation of the horse bus services. While only a minority of townsfolk would have had first hand experience of developments in other towns, a realisation would have been spreading that street tramways were becoming firmly established in many places. Indeed, as already noted, that of Gloucester was but a few miles distant, while a few more miles to the north of the town, Worcester's horse-drawn system had commenced operation in 1882. When a new approach was eventually made to the Cheltenham Corporation in 1896, the electric tramway era had arrived and the sponsor was to find that he needed only to push gently at a door which was by then showing rather more willingness to open.

The approach came from Mr Thomas Nevins, an Irish-American who gave his address as Nevins Park, Gorey, in Ireland. Nevins had established himself as an entrepreneur in the United States, where he had invested heavily and successfully in various enterprises including railways and gas supplies. His success had been based in part on his philosophy of making supplies and services available at affordable costs to the masses, and deriving increased profits from high turnover – an early exponent of what was later to become known as the 'pile it high and sell it cheap' marketing philosophy. In July 1896 the council's Streets and Highways Committee considered his request to be allowed to construct an electric tramway from a point to be agreed in Leckhampton Road to the Rising Sun Hotel on Cleeve Hill. The progress made at that meeting was extraordinarily rapid as not only was the proposal welcomed, but the Town Clerk was tasked with the drafting of a provisional agreement. The council's preference was for the line to run from Leckhampton Road along Bath Road, Grosvenor Street, Albion Street, Hewlett Road, Cemetery Road (or All Saints Road), and Prestbury Road. This was really a most extraordinary choice as it omitted the town centre altogether! (The stretch beyond Prestbury Road – through Prestbury village, Southam and Cleeve Hill – was not within the jurisdiction of the Cheltenham Corporation; Gloucestershire County Council was the highways' authority for these more rural areas).

At a meeting of the Town Council later that month, Councillor Lenthall spoke enthusiastically for the scheme, in particular for the opportunity it would give the townsfolk to travel with ease to the commons on top of the hill. He quoted the late Dr Wright: 'Cleeve (Hill) should be to Cheltenham what Clifton is to Bristol'. Some members of the council were less than convinced, but the meeting noted that although the prospect of overhead wires running through their streets was not an attractive prospect, it was an inevitable part of what they agreed would be a valuable amenity for the folk of the town. A report of the meeting prompted a response from 'Underground' in the local press advising readers that it was possible to have an electric tramway without overhead wires. He went on to cite Blackpool as an excellent example of a system drawing power from underground cables with 'absolutely no danger to thousands who walk across the lines each day'.

Just three days after the committee had expressed their preference over the route the line should follow, the Town Council, after some discussion, took the view that the route from Leckhampton should follow Bath Road as far as Cheltenham College. It should then turn along Montpellier Terrace to the Gordon Lamp, travelling on via Bayshill and the GWR station to Clarence Street, High Street and Portland Street.

At the August meeting of the Town Council, Councillors Norman and Lawrence reported favourably on a visit they had made to view the tramways in operation in both Bristol and Coventry. A letter was read from Mr Nevins justifying his decision to construct the tramway to the standard gauge of 4ft $8\frac{1}{2}$ins rather than to a gauge of 3ft 6ins as the council would have preferred. He claimed that the narrower gauge would give insufficient power for the cars to be able to climb the hill. The council noted his comments but were still uneasy on two counts. Firstly, as some of the town's streets were rather narrow, they were concerned that the tramway would present an obstruction to other users. Secondly, but of no less concern, was the prospect, should standard gauge track be approved, of freight business being generated by the through running of wagons from railway sidings in the town. The latter was now becoming more of an issue, as a third preferred route was at this point recorded. It passed both of the town's main railway stations: from the Midland Railway (MR) Station at Lansdown the line would run via Queen's Road, Lansdown Place, Bayshill Road, the Great Western Railway (GWR) Station (St James), and the town centre to Prestbury Road. Nevins attended the committee's November meeting in order to make it clear that the deal would not proceed if a standard gauge line could not be laid. While Nevins offered an assurance that passenger traffic alone would be carried between 9 a.m. and 10 p.m., this effectively served to confirm the council's suspicion of his intention to carry freight, if only during what would otherwise have remained the silent hours! He agreed however that construction of the line would be in accordance with the corporation's specifications as far as foundations, pitching and paving were concerned. The prospect of a formal agreement that would give the council the periodic option of purchasing the system was first raised at this meeting.

As the council gradually found more aspects of the proposals about which to be concerned, they were exhorted by a letter published in the *Echo* not to be dissuaded from pressing ahead with the proposals. 'WJH' wrote to say that he hoped

the Streets and Highways Committee will not be led astray by the fads and crotchets of a few fossils belonging to a bygone age. If you hire a carriage, when you reach the foot of the hill the driver will almost certainly ask you to alight and walk which sometimes under an almost tropical sun and a swarm of flies round your head is anything but a pleasing experience.

At the final council meeting of 1896 there was speculation that Nevins had been developing plans to 'move cattle, heavy goods including boilers, pig iron and machinery up to 8 tons' over the system and that he was now planning junctions with both the MR and GWR lines. There was also the possibility that the line might now run on beyond Cleeve Hill to Winchcombe, four miles distant. In order to call Nevins' bluff, the Cheltenham Corporation suggested a gauge of 4ft 6ins as a compromise; this would disbar the use of the track for railway wagons but give Nevins the advantages he was seeking of a broader gauge. It was made clear to Nevins that under no circumstances would steam power be contemplated.

The first meeting of 1897 was rather more conciliatory. Nevins had insisted on a direct connection with the GWR and the council now agreed to this on the basis that it was for parcels traffic only. There was also a compromise over the proposed frequency of the service – the Cheltenham Corporation had previously indicated that there should be a car every thirty minutes, but a subtle change in the wording to indicate that two cars would run every hour was acceptable to all parties. The proposal now was for a terminus at the GWR station, with the cars travelling along Manchester Street, Clarence Street, North Street, Albion Street, Portland Street, Clarence Road, past Pittville Gates and into Prestbury Road.

With constant reassessment of the preferred course of the line through the urban area, the benefit of hindsight can only lead to consideration as to whether the system was in effect a solution without a true requirement. While the common aim of all of the schemes was to provide a line to Cleeve Hill, it is far from clear what section of the community was to be catered for within the town. The scheme eventually adopted had the merit not only of linking the town's three main rail stations, but also of providing a service through some of the less affluent, but by no means poor, areas of the town. While the route as finally constructed was probably as logical as any single line could have been, there has to be room for speculation as to how far self-interest contributed to the long delay in determining what this route might be. While most councillors were keen to be associated with the bestowing of such a beneficial facility on the town, it did indeed appear that many of them were not in favour of the tramway running along the roads in which their houses or businesses were located. Accusations of such self-interest were to surface during acrimonious exchanges at a council meeting in 1901 (see Chapter 4). Nimbyism was clearly alive and well in the Victorian age!

The following month the council began to develop its thinking on clauses to be included in the Provisional Order. Among them were conditions imposing a maximum speed limit of 8mph, sole dependency upon electric power and a maximum width restriction such that no carriage would be allowed to overhang the rails by more than 11in. The concern over electric power dependency was two-fold – this clause would rule out any use of steam-driven trams, such as were in use in a number of towns, while at the same time guaranteeing a major boost to the sale of electricity generated by the corporation's own plant. The constraint over the width of the cars was a precaution against standard gauge railway goods wagons being carried through the streets on narrow gauge tramway trolleys. For its part, Gloucestershire County Council was insistent that no part of the line should be built outside the town until the sponsor had obtained the necessary Order to cover the full length of the line to Winchcombe. The Cheltenham Corporation opposed this stance as they feared it could delay the construction of the line to the Rising Sun.

Despite all of the generally constructive and fairly rapid progress, and for reasons which remain obscure, matters were then put on hold. It was to be a further year before the subject was further discussed, and only then as a result of approaches from other potential promoters.

In April 1898, the Cheltenham Corporation received an expression of interest in providing a tramway system in the town from Mr R. Bickerdike of Montreal, Canada. He was invited to submit a proposal; when it arrived a few weeks later it was in the form of an offer to 'build, equip and operate a system of electric railways on the trolley plan forming a complete service for the town and suburbs free of charge'. In return he asked only that the council would grant him exclusive rights, and for the company's cars and plant to be free of taxation. At the same time Nevins confirmed his interest in renewing his earlier application for the line between Cheltenham and Winchcombe – at least from the GWR station to Winchcombe 'via Bishop's

Cleeve' – the latter presumed to be a loose reference to Cleeve Hill. Within a few weeks other expressions of interest arrived from the Electric Works Co. and British Electric Tramways. It was therefore agreed that the council sub-committee should visit the newly opened system in Kidderminster, and possibly that in Coventry also. Following a visit to the Worcestershire town in July of that year, the committee members duly reported that they had been much pleased. The Town Council decided to give preference to Nevins' proposals in view of the progress achieved in 1896; the council however reserved the right to specify rates and conditions.

As the year progressed, serious work began on drafting the Provisional Order. This was the first formal step in the authorisation process laid down by the Light Railways Act of 1896; while the Tramways Act of 1870 remained in force, the procedures laid down by the Light Railways Act were possibly chosen as they appear to have been rather less tortuous. Although the 1896 Act was not specifically intended to deal with tramways, several such systems were in fact authorised under its provisions. The granting of the Provisional Order, and the eventual inspection and certification of the line was in the gift of the Light Railway Commissioners, operating under the jurisdiction of the Board of Trade. During January 1899, members of the council's newly formed Electric Tramways Committee inspected the route from Lansdown Castle to the Prestbury Road boundary. They had received 230 objections to the proposals, but at the next meeting of the council these were dismissed on the optimistic assumption that 'with a little trouble a list of 23,000 in favour could easily be compiled'! By this time the gauge had been fixed at 3ft 6in; Nevins was backing away from his previous insistence that standard gauge be adopted, probably a tactical move on his part in view of the competition which had surfaced in recent months. He had one final attempt to get his way on this important question in June 1899, but the matter then appears to have been dropped.

At this time there remained a possibility of the line running beyond Cleeve Hill to the village of Winchcombe. But as the months went by it would have become clearer that within just a few years Winchcombe would be blessed with a direct GWR link with Cheltenham, in addition to the already well-established horse bus service operated by the Gardner family. The extension to Winchcombe was not mentioned in any subsequent discussions.

The name of Cheltenham and District Light Railway Co. first appears in the minutes of the February 1899 council meeting. Although the company had been formed by Nevins towards the end of the previous year; it was under this name that the draft of the Provisional Order was finally approved by the council on 21st of that month, in readiness for submission to the Commissioners. In July of that year, the Commissioners agreed to forward the Provisional Order in respect of the stretch of line from Pittville to Cleeve Hill to the Board of Trade for ratification. The remainder of the planned route required further work as an objection had been received to the use of a short length of Wellington Road, which was in private ownership. Despite all of their differences to date, Nevins was commended by the Electric Tramways Committee for his success thus far. The Order was however further delayed as it emerged that the submission did not fully take into account all of the Town Council's observations. Council members were therefore invited to attend a meeting with the Board of Trade at which the remaining points were resolved. The Order in respect of the $3\frac{1}{2}$-mile stretch of line from Cleeve Hill to Pittville Circus was finally approved on 23 June 1899 and capital expenditure of £36,000 was fixed for that section.

Attention had turned to the remaining stretch of line, from Pittville to the GWR and MR stations. Members of the Electric Tramways Committee resolved to give Nevins their full support over the provision of this line; when their report was presented to the full Town Council it met with 'strenuous applause'. Even at this late stage, new ideas over the route were emerging; plans had recently been announced for an additional GWR station at Malvern Road, serving the new line under construction from Stratford-on-Avon via Winchcombe. The Town Council therefore proposed that the Queen's Road route be scrapped, with trams now travelling from the GWR station at St James, via St George's Road, Gloucester Road (passing the end of Malvern Road) to the MR station at Lansdown. The earlier problems relating to the planned stretch of line along Wellington Road had now been overcome by adjusting the route which would instead follow Prestbury Road, continue into Winchcombe Street and then turn into Albion Street.

The Town Council supported the carefully balanced line taken by its sub-committee; the agreed position was that of seeking to introduce all appropriate safeguards for the town in the Order, while at the same time doing everything reasonably possible to ensure that the tramway would be a commercial success. They also resolved to guard against any inconvenience or difficulty to townsfolk during the line's construction. Local churches sought assurances that there would be no tramway operation on Sunday mornings. They were eventually persuaded that the townsfolk themselves should decide whether they wished to travel to church by tram; if no-one used Sunday morning tram services, then they would be quickly withdrawn on commercial grounds.

The 2¼ mile stretch of line from Pittville Circus to Lansdown Castle was the subject of a public enquiry held in Cheltenham by the Board of Trade on 12 January 1900. Technically this part of the line was now regarded as an extension to that approved the previous year. As all points of contention had been removed through prior negotiation, the Order was granted without difficulty at the end of a hearing lasting only eighty-five minutes. Capital expenditure of £21,000 was agreed.

With the major legal points all resolved and the appropriate Orders in place, the work of both the council and Nevins' team turned to more practical matters concerning construction. There were to be many disagreements over the years with regard to the type of paving to be used between the tracks, not only before and during construction, but also when repairs were required. While these generated much debate, they are of little consequence in the context of the overall complexities of the construction phase which was about to begin.

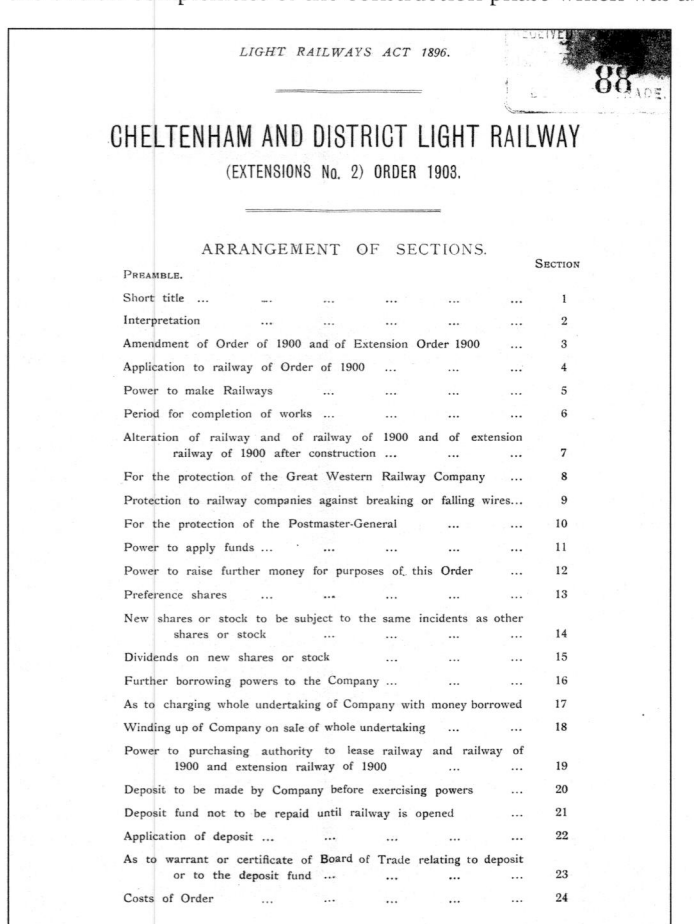

LIGHT RAILWAYS ACT 1896.

CHELTENHAM AND DISTRICT LIGHT RAILWAY

(EXTENSIONS No. 2) ORDER 1903.

ARRANGEMENT OF SECTIONS.

	Section
Preamble.	
Short title ...	1
Interpretation ...	2
Amendment of Order of 1900 and of Extension Order 1900 ...	3
Application to railway of Order of 1900 ...	4
Power to make Railways ...	5
Period for completion of works ...	6
Alteration of railway and of railway of 1900 and of extension railway of 1900 after construction ...	7
For the protection of the Great Western Railway Company ...	8
Protection to railway companies against breaking or falling wires...	9
For the protection of the Postmaster-General ...	10
Power to apply funds ...	11
Power to raise further money for purposes of this Order ...	12
Preference shares ...	13
New shares or stock to be subject to the same incidents as other shares or stock ...	14
Dividends on new shares or stock ...	15
Further borrowing powers to the Company ...	16
As to charging whole undertaking of Company with money borrowed	17
Winding up of Company on sale of whole undertaking ...	18
Power to purchasing authority to lease railway and railway of 1900 and extension railway of 1900 ...	19
Deposit to be made by Company before exercising powers ...	20
Deposit fund not to be repaid until railway is opened ...	21
Application of deposit ...	22
As to warrant or certificate of Board of Trade relating to deposit or to the deposit fund ...	23
Costs of Order ...	24

Chapters 2 and 4 make various references to Orders being made under the terms of the Light Railways Act of 1896. Many readers may be unaware of the scope of the Act; this contents sheet for one of the extension Orders in respect of Cheltenham's tramways gives an indication of the range of issues covered by the approval process. The dark patches at the top of the page are the imprints made by the official wax seals.

Three

The Plans Become Reality

During 1900, the corporation made plans to upgrade its electricity generation capability. New generating plant was installed in Manchester Street (now known as Clarence Street – where the imposing building housing the sub-station still stands on the corner of St George's Place), and the rates for the supply of electricity to the Light Railway Co. were agreed. By May 1901, the council was able to announce that all was now ready for the supply of power to the tramway system.

At their meeting on 19 October 1900, the Electric Tramways Committee heard from Nevins that he had placed orders for the cars, poles, rail, wire, etc. They were also able to view a photograph of a Liverpool car, similar to the proposed design for Cheltenham. The committee was generally content with the design, but insisted that the enclosed lower saloons of the town's cars should be fitted with opening windows. A press release, in acknowledging that the choice of right ascending stairs, generally known as 'reversed', was unusual, justified this choice on the grounds that this layout provided 'greater security, is pleasanter for ladies, allows greater carrying capacity and protects the driver from the weather'.

Towards the end of 1900, an Elder Dempster liner left the United States bound for Avonmouth with a consignment from the Loraine Steel Co. The GWR was entrusted with the onward movement of these materials to Cheltenham where they arrived in St James' goods yard on 26 January 1901. They comprised two miles of rails (weighing 85lbs per yard), fish plates, tie rods and bolts. At about the same time, Henry McCormick, a nephew of Mrs Nevins, left his home in New York and moved to Cheltenham to take up appointment as construction engineer with the Light Railway Co. Once the system became operational, he became manager, and remained with the company until his retirement thirty-one years later.

Work began in February at Cleeve Hill and by 27 April, five miles of line had been laid. There were 120 men employed on this construction project, many of them brought from the United States; their main item of equipment was a steam roller fitted with a 'devil' to assist in breaking up the more resistant surfaces. Twelve 'turn-outs' (passing loops) were being incorporated, at approximately every 2,600ft. Standards began to be erected from the end of May, at a regular interval of 120ft on straight sections. The feeder cables were laid about 18in below the road surface over the entire length of the route. The position of all points and standards required the approval of the Town Council. There was, however, little disagreement apart from the repositioning at the planning stage of a few standards in Gloucester Road. The council had specified rather ornate standards for use within the town, but those beyond the borough boundary were of a much simpler design.

On 3 June the Town Council was informed that the cars were arriving in the town and that construction of the whole line from Lansdown Castle to Cleeve Hill was proceeding well. The system was now expected to open early in July following the mandatory Board of Trade inspection; the latter was however deferred at a late stage until 31 July, almost certainly because of construction delays. Short cuts were being taken to get everything ready and early in July the town's Streets and Highways Committee had cause to reprimand Nevins for allowing rubble and other spoil to be left in the streets.

By 12 July, however, spirits began to rise, as the first car ran on test – a photograph of no.4 passing Lansdown Station on this trial run appeared in the local press. But the mood was to change dramatically when an accident on Cleeve Hill on Monday July 29 cost the lives of two of Nevins's staff. Thomas Nevins and a team of tramway staff had re-railed car no.4 in Prestbury following a derailment during a trial run. Nevins' son had been on board but had travelled back to the depot in a second car, which had come to assist; Nevins himself travelled on in the re-railed car. It stopped in Southam where several members of the public were allowed to board 'at their own risk', as no Board of Trade certificate had been granted at that time. The car was driven by an employee of Westinghouse, the electrical engineers who Nevins had called in to investigate an apparent malfunction in the car's motors. Eye witnesses reported that the car had climbed the hill at a good pace. After briefly stopping half way up the gradient, at which point Nevins had alighted, it began to slip backwards down the hill, accelerating all the way to a speed estimated to be approaching 40mph. The car's brakes were locked on and the wheels were allegedly not turning, with the car simply skidding down the track. Just after rounding the bend at the foot of the steepest section as it approached Southam, the car toppled over without warning. Two workmen standing on the car's front step were crushed as the car fell on top of them; they had been unable to jump clear as the step had given way, trapping their feet as the car began to topple. Apart from minor cuts and bruises the others on the car miraculously escaped without injury. Playing down the incident, Nevins stated that repairs had cost only £3, being limited to the replacement of one broken window and the making good of some scratches to the paintwork. (There is reference elsewhere to the car's wheels having been worn flat; it is to be hoped that those too were replaced!)

Nevins had previously determined that iron brakes were likely to be inadequate on the hill and his son had made a brake which would 'press on wheels and the earth together'. But this wooden slipper brake had not been fitted on the car at the time of the accident. The inquest held a week later into the loss of his staff returned verdicts of accidental death. Rather surprisingly, they congratulated Nevins on having previously identified a need for additional brakes, and declined the coroner's invitation to pass any further recommendations to the Board of Trade.

However the tragedy did have a lasting effect in the form of a condition imposed by the Board of Trade that passengers must not be carried on the top decks of cars on the stretch of line between Southam and Cleeve Hill. Those who had travelled on the open deck as far as Southam and wished to make the ascent were required to move downstairs when the cars stopped in that village; at busy times an extra car was used as a shuttle between Southam and Cleeve Hill. When single-deckers became available the following year, one was employed more-or-less permanently on this shuttle service.

As noted above, the formal Board of Trade inspection had been scheduled for July 31 and was to have been conducted by Col. von Donop (Royal Engineers) with Mr A.P. Trotter as the electrical adviser. In view of the tragedy, von Donop deferred his inspection of track and plant until 15 August but Trotter kept to his original schedule and was able to give seemingly unqualified approval to the electrical installation – essentially the underground cables and overhead wires. When von Donop arrived for his deferred appointment, car no.5 was awaiting him at 9.30 a.m. outside the Midland Station. On board were representatives of the Town Council, Cheltenham Rural District Council, Gloucestershire County Council, the Gloucestershire Constabulary, Westinghouse and the Light Railway Co. itself. The inspector initially examined the car, its motors and brakes in fine detail, before it set off at 9.45 a.m. After many stops along the route to inspect the track, Prestbury was reached at 10.45 a.m. Part way up the hill the newly fitted slipper brake was inspected and found to be satisfactory. At 11.05 a.m., the Rising Sun was reached at the top of the climb up the gradient which at its most severe was assessed as 1 in 8.9. There was one dewirement on the return journey, this subsequently being abandoned in the town centre as a straw cart had overturned across the line! Von Donop needed to return quickly to the MR station in order to keep an important appointment elsewhere. Although the straw cart had prevented his completing the journey by tramcar, he was nevertheless able to report before he left that he would recommend to the Board of Trade that they should pass the line as fit for use. It was immediately announced that public services would start at 10 a.m. the following Saturday, 17 August 1901.

The formal opening ceremony took place on Thursday 22 August. The public were reminded that although they had been travelling on the line for the previous few days 'it had not been dedicated to public use by decent and reasonable ceremonial, and no libations had been poured forth to the spirit of good luck'. Nearly 100 gentlemen representing local councils, companies and other organisations had been invited by the Light Railway Co. *The Cheltenham Chronicle* reported that 'two cars, gaily decorated with Union Jacks and the Stars and Stripes were in waiting for the company at the Lansdown Castle terminus at 5 p.m., and laden with their human freight, they made a triumphal progress through town and country, the people turning out in large numbers to see them 'sail' smoothly past.' The cars, nos 1 and 7, halted at the foot of Cleeve Hill and the party assembled in a nearby field where champagne was served for all to join the mayor in a toast: 'Success to the Light Railway'. Curiously, the cars did not proceed further up the hill, but returned to town, experiencing on the way an embarrassing power outage which delayed them for some minutes at Pittville Villas. The guests reassembled that evening for a dinner in the Winter Gardens at which a number of toasts accompanied further congratulatory speeches delivered to members of both the Light Railway Co. and the Town Council. Congratulations did indeed appear in order as over 40,000 paying passengers had travelled on the system in its first full seven days of operation!

As construction of the line proceeded, the Light Railway Co. had also been establishing its base on a large site near the MR station; a shed was built to accommodate the cars, along with an office for the manager. This depot, always to be known as St Mark's, was connected to the main system by several hundred yards of single-track line laid along its approach road which ran alongside the main Birmingham-bound Midland Railway line.

Like much of the equipment, the initial eight open-top double-deck cars had also been sourced from the United States, where they were manufactured by the J. Stephenson Car Co. in New York. They had been shipped over in a partly dismantled state and assembled on arrival at St Mark's; it seems likely that the lower saloons were shipped more-or-less intact but that the staircases and somewhat rudimentary upper deck fittings were transported separately. Once completed, the bodies were mounted on Peckham trucks. The cars had open vestibules. The longitudinal lower deck seats for eleven passengers each side were upholstered, while those for twenty-six on the open deck were of the customary slatted wooden variety with adjustable seat backs. By sliding the backs from one side of the seat to the other, passengers could always be seated facing the direction of travel. Although the Town Council had previously asked that the cars be painted in red with blue relief, Nevins had simplified this to a single colour – dark red. The names of the company (in full), the town arms and the fleet number were prominently displayed in gold lettering on both sides of the cars. The upper deck passengers were 'protected' only by wire mesh extending to a level equivalent to seat height, and a guard rail at shoulder height (when seated). The single headlamps were also mounted at top deck level. There was no destination equipment, this being largely unnecessary for the single route for which they had been acquired. Power was collected from the overhead wires via sprung trolley arms, these being mounted on the trolley-posts located at one side of the top deck.

Recruitment of drivers had proved not to be a problem; a number of local men had responded to the company's advertisements while some experienced motormen transferred from Bristol, on which system there had been recent industrial unrest.

Thus, at last, electric trams were running in Cheltenham.

The four views on these pages are of car no.5 during the official inspection on 15 August 1901. The small party of official guests had started their journey in company with the Board of Trade Inspector, Colonel von Donop, at the Midland Station and travelled along the line to Cleeve Hill, stopping at regular intervals for aspects of construction to be examined. Interestingly the American-built car has been equipped with neither its upper deck seats, nor its staircases. The car is seen above at the Cleeve Hill terminus. Standing in the centre of the group is Colonel von Donop. Next to him (to the right in this view) is Mr Thomas Nevins. The County Surveyor (Mr R Phillips) and the Borough Surveyor (Mr J Hall) stand nearer to the car and Mr T A Nevins (Thomas's son) is in the background. Some passing cyclists were no doubt thrilled to be witnessing one of the first cars to run up the hill. In the photograph below the car is beginning the descent. Note the unmade road surface, and the track positioned well over to the side of the road, as it was for the whole of the rural stretch. (All: Gloucestershire Echo)

The cyclists have followed the car down the hill and caught up with it again as it stands in the passing loop at Southam; this was of course then on the main road, the short stretch of road through the village not having been by-passed until the 1960s.

As the car returned through the town centre, the heads of most passers-by turned to admire the town's new attraction. The cut-out may be clearly seen in the floor of the upper deck where the staircase would have shortly been installed.

Car no. 4 is seen while awaiting the fitting of its top deck seats before entering service in August 1901; the staircases have however already been installed. The photograph was presumably taken at St Mark's depot; if this is indeed the case, the building to the right is probably the original tram shed. The depot needed a major rebuild in 1905 when the new cars arrived for the Charlton Kings and Leckhampton routes. Note the all-over dark red livery; this was however relieved by the company's name displayed in full, the Cheltenham arms, and neat lining-out of the main panels. The staff on board were probably those involved in assembling and fitting out the original eight cars following their arrival from the United States.

The Gloucestershire Echo's photographer captured the same car a few days later as it passed along Gloucester Road, outside the Midland Station, when on a test run before the system had been opened to the public. A select few are enjoying themselves on the upper deck while on the platform two people look intently at the controls; quite probably the driver was under instruction. In this view the four side windows of these early cars are clearly visible. The sparse upper deck fittings may also be seen.

A grand ceremony accompanied the official launch of the system on Thursday 22 August 1901. Around 100 invited guests joined cars 1 and 7 at Lansdown Castle for a triumphant trip to Southam, at the foot of Cleeve Hill, and back to the town centre. The cars are seen here, suitably bedecked with both British and American flags, with their influential guests already on board, ready to set off across town. The system had in fact already been in use by the public for over a week following the official inspection, and during that time no fewer than 40,000 paying passengers had been carried. The headlights in these cars were mounted at top-deck level, as may be clearly seen in this view. (Gloucestershire Echo)

Later on the same day, car no.7 is seen at Southam; the guests had moved into a nearby field to enjoy a champagne celebration in which a number of passers-by were also invited to join. Rather curiously the official party had not travelled beyond Southam.

A surprising number of viewcards containing either deliberate or chance images of Cheltenham's trams were produced during the early part of the 20th century. Cleeve Hill was always a popular setting for such views. Here car no.7 rests at the terminus at the top of the 1-in-8.9 climb up from Southam.

Car no.3 passes the junction of Prestbury Road and Pittville Circus Road, probably in the summer of 1902, returning from Cleeve Hill. Note how full the car is; those standing upstairs are either in breach of the company's bye-laws (see pages 46 & 47) or are more likely queuing to follow others down the stairs.

Cars nos 8 (nearest the camera) and 6 are seen near the Hales Road junction on the route to Charlton Kings which opened in 1905. The long double-track section, which commenced immediately to the south of The Strand, ended at this point. At the time of the photograph this stretch of road was still known as High Street, but in more recent times has been re-named London Road. Both cars are in the later livery. The unmetalled road surface and the ankle-length dress of the shop assistant suggest that this view dates from the pre-First World War period.

Two of the early cars, with no.2 on the right, on the passing loop at North Street, outside the Globe Inn. The Globe stood next door to the tramway's office, which doubled as a waiting room for the Cleeve Hill service. This view probably dates from the first year of operation of the system as both cars are in their original condition, without the upper-deck decency panels added soon after 1902. In the left foreground a workman undertakes a rudimentary repair to the unmetalled road surface. Number 2 is featured in all four views on this and the facing page.

PITVILLE GATES, CHELTENHAM.

Although the viewcard has been somewhat retouched, and once again shows car no.2, this time passing Pittville Gates, it is of interest as it shows the span wires necessary to support the overhead on corners such as this. A plain pole is used on the left while one of the ornamental standards stands on the pavement on the right. The card is post-marked 1907 but the photograph will probably date from the 1902-1905 period; the approximate date may be calculated from the fitting of decency panels, the retention of the early all-red livery, and the lack of destination boxes.

Two further views of car no. 2. Both are of the same side, as may be determined from the position of the side-mounted trolley pole. In the photograph above, probably at the Lansdown Castle terminus, the car displays the same characteristics as in the view (opposite) at Pittville Gates, so again the date must be c.1902-1905. Enamelled advertising signs have been applied in most cases, although that on the main side panel for John Lance is advertising his Great Sale and was therefore almost certainly a temporary paper poster. Two small adverts appear to the right of that panel and Williams, Clare and Co. have taken the panels on either side of the headlight. The reversed staircase, curving up over the driver's head, may be clearly seen. In the photograph below at the Lilleybrook terminus, outside the New Inn, the car, with destination boxes now in place, is seen in the later livery, with cream relief and with the more rounded style of fleet numbers which appeared later in the cars' lives. Farrar's Coals, in business until the 1970s, had by this time taken the main advertising space.

Sister car no. 10, also on Cleeve Hill. This view shows clearly the common on top of the hill, access to which for the growing population of Cheltenham provided the main impetus for the original construction of the line. The photograph also shows the reserved track created for the tramway at the side of the main road over the hill to Winchcombe. The line of the original grass verge may be seen beyond the car. In the right foreground, outside the Malvern View Hotel, drainage works are underway. Like no. 9 above, the car has roof-mounted destination boxes and is in the later livery. The date is probably c.1910.

Cleeve Hill, Tram Terminus, Cheltenham

Of the four cars sourced locally in 1902 from the Gloucester Railway Carriage and Wagon works, two were single-deckers. Nos 9 and 10 spent most of their lives shuttling between Southam and Cleeve Hill, taking passengers off the double-deckers at the passing loop in Southam village. Here no.9 is seen at Cleeve Hill terminus.

The other two 1902 cars were double-deckers, built to the same style as the original 1901 cars, and sharing their main identification features: the inclusion of four windows on each side of the lower saloon, the side-mounted trolley poles, reversed staircases and high-level headlights. Here no.11 passes along the High Street, in quite a contrast to the Cleeve Hill views on the previous page. The line along this stretch, between the junctions at Cambray and North Street, was double-track; two cars head for the centre, presumably one from Leckhampton and the other from Charlton Kings. The more distant car is no.13, one of the 1905 delivery. A single motor car is in evidence, suggesting the view pre-dates the First World War.

A posed view of car no.12 when it was newly delivered in 1902. Note the plywood decency boards surrounding the upper deck, the only significant visual difference from the 1901 cars – and one which soon disappeared as the original cars were also so equipped. The small opening windows on which the Cheltenham Corporation insisted may be seen clearly above the main glazed panes. The photograph was taken outside the Midland Hotel, so named as it stands directly opposite the Midland Station.

Tramway enthusiasts now use the term 'the last car' to refer to the final car to run as a tramway system was closing down. A century ago, the term simply referred to the last car of the day. Cards such as this were produced for many locations. That a tramcar should be used as the subject of such an offering in the early years of the last century indicates perhaps that, while the cars were much used and undoubtedly appreciated, as with any public service they were also the butt of many jokes. The card is post-marked 1908.

Four

More New Lines in Prospect

Just as Nevins' initial line in Cheltenham was about to be opened to the public, he was given a rapturous welcome in July 1901 at a meeting held in the village of Painswick, twelve miles distant. He had begun to consider the possibility of a line from Cheltenham to Stroud, passing through the village, whose residents were most enthusiastic about the prospect of an enhancement of their occasional horse bus service. The proposal was developed through various stages and a Provisional Order was approved in 1902 in the name of the Stroud District and Cheltenham Tramways. The plans were reduced in scope in 1903 to serve only the Stroud – Painswick section of the route, a move to which Cheltenham Town Council raised strong objections. In the event the scheme, even in its truncated form, did not proceed.*(See also pages 44 & 45)*.

At about the same time as he was thinking about the Stroud possibilities, Nevins also began to consider further lines within Cheltenham. At the October 1901 meeting of the Electric Tramways Committee, the Light Railway Co. suggested that lines might now be considered to both Charlton Kings and Leckhampton. The company cited 'numerous applications from residents' by way of support. In noting the company's aspirations, the committee for their part passed on to the company complaints received from the public over punctuality on the existing lines!

At the October meeting of the Town Council a lengthy debate took place over the possibility of entertaining the future extensions. There were three main issues. The first concerned the line of the original routes which had failed to be as useful as they might have been due to the prejudices of council members – a full frontal attack on the nimbyism referred to earlier. The second issue was unsatisfactory maintenance of the existing lines, coupled both with unease over punctuality and dissatisfaction over fares. An overarching issue however was that of 'municipalisation'; this topic was to rumble on for the next seventy years and on many occasions led to lively debate within the council chamber. One school strongly represented the view that the council ought to own and operate the town's transport system itself in order to be more responsive to the needs and concerns of the public, while ensuring that any profits would be used for their full benefit rather than lining the pockets of the shareholders of a commercial organisation. Others supported equally vociferously the opposing view that the council was not well placed to manage such an operation and that it would not realistically be able to raise the necessary capital sums for either the initial purchase or the appropriate level of future investment. They also recognised the advantages of being able to take a second party to task when things went wrong. A touch of additional colour was introduced to these frequent debates by those still unhappy with the arrival of the tramways in Cheltenham. On one occasion they were described as being an eyesore, of no public convenience and of no utility in a town like Cheltenham! The continued healthy loadings on the cars might however suggest that this particular councillor was not representing the views of those who had put him in office.

The concerns over the route of the original line are interesting. In reality it seems likely that the right route was chosen, albeit for the wrong reasons. The criticism was probably a reflection of the view that travelling via Gloucester Road and St George's Road represented a longer and slower journey between the MR station and the town centre than the original plan to travel via Queen's Road and Bayshill. In fact those relatively affluent areas would probably have generated little in the way of custom for Nevins' creation. It is interesting to observe that, one hundred years later and for good commercial reasons, most of the bus services between the railway station and the Centre still follow the route of those original trams.

The conclusion of that October meeting was such that at its next gathering the Electric Tramways Committee was able to give agreement in principle to the new lines. It was, though, made clear to the company that these would only be considered in any depth once the existing lines had been brought up to the required standards, some fares had been modified and some additional passing places had been constructed in order to improve punctuality. Without allowing himself to be distracted by such tedious matters, Nevins delivered plans for the proposed extensions to the committee's December meeting. The town surveyor and electrical engineer had meanwhile drawn up schedules of the work needed to bring the existing lines up to the required standards. The committee dropped an earlier demand for double-track to be provided along St George's Road, and agreed instead on a modification to the passing loops in that road.

In January 1902, the borough surveyor presented a very damning report on the state of the town's tramway system, which he described as one of the most badly constructed lines in England. In defence of the company it was pointed out that the most common cause of failure was that of the council's electricity supply! The paving bricks which had caused most difficulty were those which had been supplied by the Cheltenham Corporation, while the others had not only been to the corporation's specification, but had also been purchased from their recommended supplier. The line itself had been constructed under the supervision of the borough surveyor. As if that defence of its position were not sufficiently robust, the company came away victorious by announcing that four more cars were to be acquired for 'hill traffic'.

It will perhaps already have become clear that Nevins was an excellent tactician. He was a particularly shrewd negotiator, always able to assess just how far he could push the council and its committees, and always careful to do just enough to avoid any serious accusations of not meeting his obligations to the town. In February 1902 he challenged the council by demanding to know whether they intended to exercise their option to purchase the system from him at the 'fair price' to which the agreement referred. This was in part precipitated by further pressure from some councillors for the town to acquire the system and manage the construction of the extensions themselves. Given the assurance he was seeking, Nevins indicated that he would be happy to continue with his plans and to meet the requirements of the committee as already agreed. In order to prevent any backsliding, the following month Nevins announced that he was placing a deposit with the council of £5,000 towards the rectification of the existing lines.

At a special meeting of the Town Council held on 13 May 1902 to reach agreement on the extensions, a minority continued to oppose the scheme. One councillor, in acknowledging that he could not resist a further dissertation on the benefits of municipalisation, went further and expressed the view that Nevins did not at that time stand in a very bright light with the council. Indeed, they had to thank him for being a party to one of the most painful incidents in the modern history of Cheltenham! In trying to restore some order, another councillor exhorted all those present to recognise that the council was in effect 'wedded to Nevins in this scheme', and that all parties should therefore work amicably together for the benefit of the town. Some skilful chairmanship was necessary to resolve eventually all outstanding issues. The Tramways Committee was however congratulated on a balanced report on the extension proposals.

The Light Railway Commissioners held a public enquiry in Cheltenham just two days later in order to examine the case for the Charlton Kings and Leckhampton extensions. Evidence was taken from a cross section of supporters and opponents of the scheme, primarily landowners and businessmen; the overwhelming conclusion was that the scheme was well founded and should be allowed to proceed. However, there was concern over the wisdom of the line passing through The Strand, the narrowest part of the High Street. The Commissioners concluded that the line must instead turn from High Street into Cambray Place and run along Bath Street into Bath Road at which point cars for Leckhampton would branch right, and those for Charlton Kings would turn left to rejoin the High Street. The Light Railway Order in respect of these extensions was accordingly issued.

In August 1902 a shock announcement was made of Thomas Nevins' sudden death. Cheltenham Town Council extended their condolences, and noted that Nevins' son, also Thomas, would be carrying on in his father's stead. Nevins junior had been working with his father throughout the development of the Cheltenham system; from what can be seen of the way that business was subsequently conducted, it can only be concluded that he had inherited his father's negotiating tactics and business acumen.

The four new cars promised by Nevins at the January 1902 meeting were constructed locally, by the Gloucester Railway Carriage and Wagon Co. They arrived in the spring of that year. These were to a broadly similar design to the original octet. Two of the new cars, nos 9 and 10, were single-deckers, while 11 and 12 were of double-deck construction; the latter pair were delivered with timber boarding covering the mesh screens around the upper deck, to give them a rather more solid and dignified appearance. The single-deckers were to be regularly deployed on the Southam-Cleeve Hill shuttle service; three seats were provided in the vestibules at either end of these two cars (where the stairs would otherwise have been located), to give them a seating capacity of twenty-eight. The double-deckers seated twenty-six on top and twenty-two below. In common with the earlier cars, the trolley masts on all four of these cars were side-mounted; no destination equipment was fitted.

At about this time, the top decks of the earlier cars also received similar upper-deck 'decency panels'. The fitting of these panels opened the way for advertisements to appear. While initially they were printed on lightweight materials, probably paper in some cases, which could be pasted on to the new panels, very soon the more conventional enamelled advertising panels were introduced, some remaining in situ for many years.

Charlton Kings and Leckhampton had both been served since 1890 by the horse bus services of the Cheltenham Omnibus Co., as explained in Chapter 1. The Omnibus Co. was quite naturally less than happy with the agreement to provide tram services to both of those districts: it had already seen its services to Prestbury and Southam displaced by the opening of the Cleeve Hill line. At a meeting on 21 September 1901 between Thomas Nevins and the directors of the Omnibus Co., the following was agreed:

i) As soon as the Board of Trade had approved the Orders for the Leckhampton and Charlton Kings routes, the Light Railway Co. would pay the sum of £500 to the Omnibus Co.

ii) The Omnibus Co. would discontinue its services in the town as soon as the Orders had been approved (if they were not already discontinued by that date).

iii) The directors of the Omnibus Co. would not set up any new operation in competition with the Light Railway Co.

iv) The Omnibus Co. would in any case be at liberty to discontinue its operations at any time after 31 October 1902.

v) Regardless of when the services might cease, the Light Railway Co. would have the option of purchasing all scheduled assets for the sum of £2,800.

vi) The Omnibus Co. would immediately withdraw from the route between Lansdown and the High Street (on which they had been competing with the trams for the past year).

In the event it appears that the operation of all horse bus services in the town ceased at the end of October 1902, for early in November, the *Cheltenham Chronicle* could not resist recording the mood of the stranded passengers in the following verse:

Standing one day in the High Street, I was weary and ill at ease;
My feet were tapping the pavement, the East wind made me sneeze.
I know well what I was thinking, and of what I was dreaming then;
I thought with regret of the two-penny 'bus, and dreamed of the coming tram.
It may be in the spring-time, after weeks of discomfort and rain,
That, thanks to Messrs Nevins, we'll get cheap locomotion again.
It may be the coming tram-car is worth all the waiting and fuss;
But why keep us all the winter without the twopenny 'bus?

Unfortunately for those deprived of their 'cheap locomotion' it was to be three more winters before the trams would come to their salvation. Nevins junior duly handed over the promised £500 on 4 June 1903 but appears to have made no attempt to purchase any of the Omnibus Co.'s assets in order to ensure continuity of operations.

Nevins' proposal for the new lines had included two additional routes not yet mentioned. One had been planned to run from the High Street/Ambrose Street junction, along the Lower High Street, past the gas works to the bridge over the Midland Railway. The second was planned to provide a connection along Gloucester Road, leaving the original line at the Calcutta and meeting the other new line at the gas works. By mid-1903 rumours abounded that these lines might not be constructed, at least not 'for the present'. Nevins was challenged over his latest intentions amidst a smoke-screen that even the Charlton Kings line was now in doubt. Nevins clarified the situation at a joint meeting of the Streets and Highways Committee and the Electric Tramways Committee on 10 September. He confirmed that he was about to let contracts for lines as follows:

1) St Gregory's Church – Ambrose Street – High Street – Cambray – Bath Street – Bath Road – High Street – London Road – borough boundary
2) Bath Street – Bath Road – Norwood Arms – Leckhampton (foot of hill).

Some explanation may be helpful. St Gregory's Church in St James' Square was already served by the original line, and would now become a junction. This new line would cross the Cleeve Hill line at the intersection of the High Street with Clarence Street and North Street, and suitable interconnecting points would be provided between them. This new Charlton Kings line would in fact extend to a terminus to be established at Lilleybrook; the route beyond the borough boundary fell within the jurisdiction of the Charlton Kings Urban District Council and was not therefore detailed in the notification to the Cheltenham Corporation. The stretches of line between St Gregory's and Cambray would be double track, as would that between the Grosvenor Street and Hales Road junctions with London Road. The Leckhampton line would diverge from the Charlton Kings line at the Bath Street/Bath Road junction and would terminate 70yds short of the junction of Leckhampton Road and Old Bath Road. Double track would run as far as the Montpellier Terrace junction.

At the Town Council meeting of 5 October 1903 Nevins provided an assurance that work would be starting within sixty days and that the new lines would be running by 1 May 1904. Having delivered that good news he was able to confirm, almost as an aside, that the Lower High Street proposals ('the Gas Works plan') had for the present been abandoned.

On 9 March 1904 a further public enquiry was held in Cheltenham by the Light Railway Commissioners to examine a proposal by the Light Railway Co. It suggested that, despite the outcome of the May 1902 enquiry, the Charlton Kings and Leckhampton trams should after all be allowed to travel through The Strand, where they now wished to construct eight chains of single-track line, instead of the deviation via Cambray Place and Bath Street. It was noted that, unlike the situation at the previous hearing, a considerable majority of traders in The Strand now favoured the line passing in front of their premises. The Cambray route involved three very tight turns, and it was argued that the low speeds of the cars in negotiating this section would cause an obstruction to other traffic. After due consideration the Commissioners ruled that Charlton Kings trams could after all travel along The Strand, but those for Leckhampton must continue to be routed via Cambray Place and Bath Street. The short length of line along Bath Road between Bath Street and High Street would not now be required and a set of points would be needed at the Cambray Place/High Street junction in place of those originally planned for the junction of Bath Street and Bath Road.

At about the same time, agreement was reached between Nevins and the Town Council that the line from St Gregory's to the centre would now be of single track construction, while the state of the existing lines was once again towards the top of the council's agenda. Nevertheless on 6 June 1904 an agreement was signed between the Town Council and the Light Railway Co. for work to begin on the extensions and for the existing lines 'to be repaired from end-to-end'.

Construction of the new lines eventually commenced on 28 September. The construction contractors were Messrs Robert W Blackwell & Co. of London, with the paving work subcontracted to the Acme Wood Paving Co. Their foreman confidently stated as work began in Leckhampton Road that the task would be completed within six months; despite a month of hard frosts he was able to keep that promise. Henry McCormick once again acted as Superintending Engineer on behalf of the Light Railway Co. He provided the following facts on the extensions to the *Gloucestershire Echo*:

Route mileage: $4\frac{1}{2}$
Track mileage: $6\frac{1}{6}$ (allowing for double track sections and passing loops)
Materials used: 1,600tons of Scottish granite sets; around 900tons of rail (in 45ft lengths, at 90lbs per yard) from Leeds; 15,500yards of English copper wire; 50tons of home-made fish plates, tiebars and bolts; many thousands of hard wood blocks of Australian Jarrah and English creosoted red deal blocks; 3miles of underground cable from Callenders; many standard poles from Wednesbury.
Labour: More than 400 men, in addition to those working for carters and hauliers.

McCormick was anxious to stress the British origins of the materials – probably an indication that there had been criticism of the high US content of the original line. He explained that on this occasion 'only small specialities' had been obtained from the Loraine Co. in the States. The total cost of construction was in the region of £50,000-£60,000, this figure including £5,000 for eight new cars, details of which are given in the next chapter. The extension of the depot and office accommodation at St Mark's was said to cost at least a further £10,000. Only two injuries were recorded during the construction work, the most serious being a broken leg allegedly caused by a passing wagon.

During construction many others issues surfaced. The alignment of the junction in the town centre (High Street/North Street/Clarence Street) was the subject of considerable debate. A dispute also arose over the responsibility for financing a realignment of the road surface in Gloucester Road, where to establish a level track the lines had in places to be raised slightly above the level of the existing road. John Lance complained bitterly that the passage of trams would cause inconvenience and loss to his business, particularly as clients would now be unable to park their carriages outside his department store in Clarence Street. In the event the council agreed to reduce the width of the pavement, to provide sufficient road width for carriages and trams to co-exist. It also came to light that councillors and council employees had been enjoying free passes for travel on the trams; it was now feared that these might be construed as an inducement to support Nevins and this potentially valuable facility was withdrawn in January 1905.

At the end of that month the Light Railway Co. informed the Streets and Highways Committee that they had asked the Board of Trade for new deadlines of 31 March for the extensions, and February 1907 for the Gas Works lines. The committee was relaxed about the former but insisted the Gas Works lines should be completed by February 1906 – although, surprisingly, they conceded that they would be prepared to reconsider later if there were still difficulties.

The Cheltenham Chronicle's *photographic supplement captured many views of the construction work on the lines to Charlton Kings and Leckhampton in the early months of 1905. The amount of disruption to other road users may be clearly seen as work progressed. On this page, from the top: the new junction alongside St Gregory's Church (with the original Clarence Street line to the right), the complex junction in the town centre with the Empress Tea Stores on the corner of High Street and North Street, and the double track section taken from the junction with Hewlett Street, now Hewlett Road, looking along the High Street.*

Work underway in High Street, now London Road, looking south from the Hewlett Street junction, and in Copt Elm Road at Charlton Kings. At the foot of the page members of the track gang, while taking a welcome break from their work, seemingly ready for a night on the town.

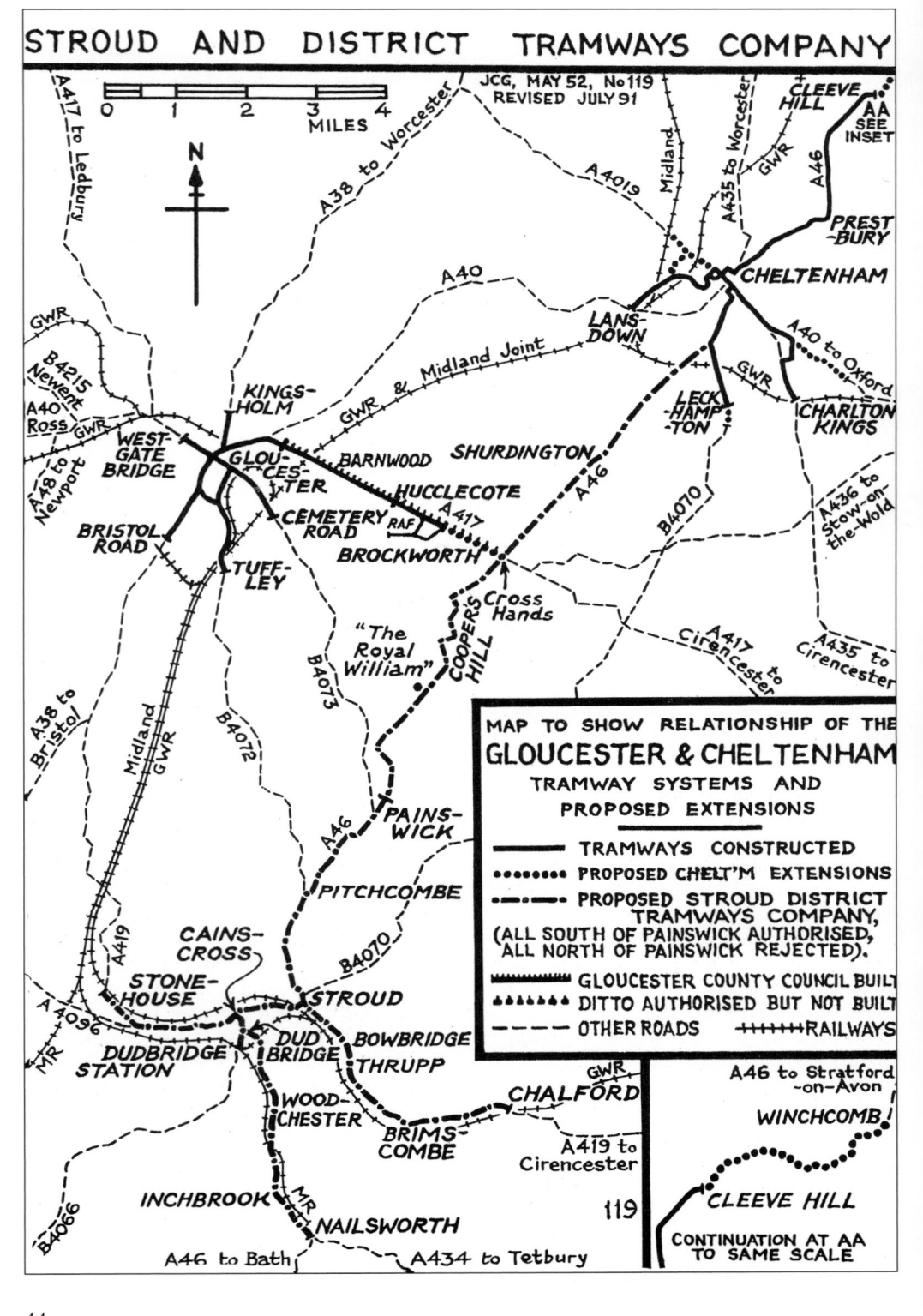

STROUD AND DISTRICT TRAMWAYS COMPANY

MAP TO SHOW RELATIONSHIP OF THE
GLOUCESTER & CHELTENHAM
TRAMWAY SYSTEMS AND
PROPOSED EXTENSIONS

TRAMWAYS CONSTRUCTED
PROPOSED CHELT'M EXTENSIONS
PROPOSED STROUD DISTRICT
TRAMWAYS COMPANY,
(ALL SOUTH OF PAINSWICK AUTHORISED,
ALL NORTH OF PAINSWICK REJECTED).
GLOUCESTER COUNTY COUNCIL BUILT
DITTO AUTHORISED BUT NOT BUILT
OTHER ROADS   RAILWAYS

JCG, MAY 52, No 119
REVISED JULY 91

CONTINUATION AT AA
TO SAME SCALE

119

44

Chapter 4 began with a brief reference to the abortive plans for a tramway connecting Cheltenham with Stroud, following the line of what subsequently became known as the A46. In the map reproduced on the opposite page, generously made available by well-known transport historian Mr John Gillham, the proposed route of that line is shown, along with its relationship with the urban tramway systems in both Cheltenham and Gloucester. The possibilities for through travel between the three lines would have made an exciting prospect. Nevins himself won the support of the Gloucestershire County Council for the construction of a connecting line from the Cross Hands junction at Brockworth into the city centre. However, following rejection by the Light Railway Commissioners of the proposals for the stretch of line north of Painswick, his Gloucester scheme became irrelevant. This much delighted Gloucester Corporation, who were themselves about to begin work on an electric tramway system within the City. They had been less than impressed with the system which Nevins had to that date constructed in Cheltenham, although there may have been an element of jealousy that their near and rather conservative neighbour had beaten them into the electric tramway age. Gloucester's electric tramways were opened to the public in May 1904. A line to Brockworth was indeed constructed, but not until 1917, when it was needed to serve the airfield which had been constructed there in support of the war effort. Shortage of materials, though, meant that the Westgate line had to be surrendered in order that its track could be reused.

The map illustrates the network which the Stroud proposals had envisaged in that town, with routes diverging to serve Nailsworth, Chalford and Stonehouse. In each case the tramways would have followed the railway lines as a consequence of the terrain, with a need for both to follow the lower ground along the valleys which characterise the Stroud area.

BYE-LAWS AND REGULATIONS

Made by the CHELTENHAM AND DISTRICT LIGHT RAILWAY COMPANY, under the Statutory Powers incorporated with the Cheltenham and District Light Railway Order, 1900

1. The Bye-Laws and Regulations hereinafter set forth shall extend and apply to all cars of the Company, and to all places with respect to which the Company have powers to make bye-laws and regulations.

2. Every passenger shall enter or depart from a car by the hindermost or conductor's platform, and not otherwise.

3. No passenger shall smoke inside any car.

4. No passenger or other person shall, while travelling in or upon any car, play or perform upon any musical instrument.

5. A person in a state of intoxication shall not be allowed to enter or mount upon any car, and if found in or upon any car shall be immediately removed by or under the direction of the conductor.

6. No person shall swear or use offensive or obscene language whilst in or upon any car, or commit any nuisance in or upon, or against, any car, or wilfully interfere with the comfort of any passenger.

7. No person shall wilfully cut, tear, soil or damage the cushions or the linings, or remove or deface any number plate, printed or other notice, in or on the car, or break or scratch any window, or otherwise wilfully damage any car. Any person acting in contravention of this regulation shall be liable to the penalty prescribed by these Bye-Laws and Regulations, in addition to the liability to pay the amount of any damage down.

8. A person whose dress or clothing might, in the opinion of the conductor of a car, soil or injure the linings or cushions of the car, or the dress or clothing of any passenger, or a person, who, in the opinion of the conductor, might for any other reason be offensive to passengers, shall not be entitled to enter or remain in the interior of any car, and may be prevented from entering the interior of the car, and shall not enter the interior of any car after having been requested not to do so by the conductor; and if found in the interior of any car, shall, on request of the conductor, leave the interior of the car upon the fare, if previously paid, being returned.

9. Each passenger shall, upon demand, pay to the conductor, or otherwise duly authorised officer of the Company, the fare legally demanded for the journey.

10. Each passenger shall show his ticket (if any), when required so to do, to the conductor, or any duly authorised servant of the Company, and shall, also, when required to do so, either deliver up his ticket or pay the fare legally demanded for the distance travelled by such passenger.

11. No luggage, other than personal luggage carried by hand, shall be brought upon any car, and all such luggage (including the tools of artisans, mechanics, or daily labourers,) shall, unless permitted by the conductor, be placed on the front or driver's platform, and not in the interior or on the roof of any car.

12. No passenger or other person, not being a servant of the Company, shall be permitted to travel on the steps or platforms of any car, or stand either on the roof or in the interior, or sit on the outside rail on the roof of any car, and shall cease to do so imediately on request by the conductor.

13. No person, except a passenger or intended passenger, shall enter or mount any car, and no person shall hold or hang on by or to any part of any car, or travel therein, otherwise than on a seat provided for passengers.

14. When any car contains the full number of passengers which it is licensed to contain, no additional person shall enter, mount, or remain in or on any such car when warned by the conductor not to do so.

15. When a car contains the full licensed number of passengers, a notice to that effect shall be placed in conspicuous letters, and in a conspicuous position on the car.

16. The conductor shall not permit any passenger beyond the licensed number to enter, or mount, or remain in or upon any part of a car.

17. No person shall enter, mount, or leave, or attempt to mount, enter, or leave any car whilst in motion.

18. No dog or other animal shall be allowed in or on any car except by permission of the conductor, or in any case in which the conveyance of such dog or other animal might be offensive or an annoyance to passengers. No person shall take a dog or other animals into any car after having been requested not to do so by the conductor. Any dog or other animal taken into or on any car, in breach of this Regulation, shall be removed by the person in charge of such dog or other animal from the car immediately upon request of the conductor and, in default of compliance with such request, may be removed by or under the direction of the conductor.

19. No person shall travel in or on any car of the Company with loaded firearms.

20. No person shall wilfully obstruct or impede any officer of the Company in the execution of his duty upon or in connection with any car or tramway of the Company.

21. The conductor of any car shall enforce or prevent the breach of these Bye-laws and Regulations to the best of his ability.

22. Any person offending against or committing a breach of any of these Bye-laws or Regulations shall be liable to a penalty not exceeding Two Pounds.

23. The expression, "conductor", shall include any officer or servant in the employ of the Company and having charge of a car.

24. There shall be placed, and kept placed, in a conspicuous position inside of each car in use, a printed copy of these Bye-Laws and Regulations.

Given under the Common Seal of the Cheltenham and District Light Railway Company, the 21st day of December, 1901, in the presence of Thomas Nevins, Chairman of the Company.

The Board of Trade hereby signify their allowance and approval of the above Bye-Laws and Regulations.

Signed by order of the Board of Trade, this 28th day of December, 1901,
Herbert Jekyll, Assistant Secretary.

The bye-laws and regulations of the Cheltenham and District Light Railway Co. were approved in draft by the Cheltenham Town Council, prior to their submission by the company for formal ratification by the Board of Trade. The final approved version, as shown here, was displayed in all of the company's cars.

The opening ceremony for the Charlton Kings and Leckhampton lines was much lower key than that for the original 1901 line. The official Board of Trade inspection was carried out on 28 March 1905. At 4 o'clock that same afternoon, the Mayor of Cheltenham set car no.13 in motion as Mr H.J. McCormick, the company's Manager and Engineer, took a party of local dignitaries on a trip over both of the new lines. Here new car no.13 is standing at the junction of High Street and Cambray waiting to set off on its celebratory trip. In the lower of these views along the High Street, another of the eight new cars is seen drawn up behind.

Five

Charlton Kings and Leckhampton Come On Line

The official Board of Trade inspection of the new lines was carried out by Maj. J.W. Pringle on 28 March 1905. With a large crowd of officials and dignitaries in attendance, new car no.13 left Cambray Place at 10.30 a.m. and returned there within thirty minutes having first travelled to the Leckhampton terminus. The same car set off again from the Cambray/High Street junction, reaching the Charlton Kings terminus at 11.24 a.m. On the return journey there was a pause after the car had turned from Lyefield Road West into Copt Elm Road as Maj. Pringle needed to be satisfied that the curve needed to be quite so sharp to achieve this ninety-degree turn. The car passed Cambray at 11.44 a.m. and travelled on along the new tracks to Ambrose Street. Maj. Pringle then asked that the car traverse the new junctions in the town centre. He alighted at 12.15 p.m. and travelled to St Mark's with McCormick and other officials where he declared himself well satisfied, indicating that he would recommend acceptance to the Board of Trade. At 4.00 p.m. McCormick took various other local dignitaries on a trip in one of the new cars to Leckhampton and to the borough boundary on the Charlton Kings line. The Mayor set the car going as it left the town centre and this was therefore in effect the official opening ceremony. The lines were opened for public service the following morning.

The new lines of course needed new cars and eight more open-top double-deckers had been delivered in good time. These had been supplied by the British Thomson-Houston Co. in Rugby, and entered service numbered 13–20. These differed from the earlier cars in some fundamental respects: they had only three windows on each side, instead of four, the trolley-masts were mounted centrally and their head-lamps were in the front dash rather than being mounted much higher in the canopy. Longitudinal cane straw seating was again fitted in the lower saloons with reversible slatted seats on top. Like the earlier cars they were mounted on Peckham trucks and fitted with Westinghouse electrical equipment. These cars were not however fitted with slipper brakes and could never therefore venture to Cleeve Hill.

After the cars were delivered a lighter livery of bright red ('lake') and cream ('primrose') was introduced when cars required repainting, and eventually applied to the whole fleet. Cars could run to any of four destinations from the centre of town, so destinations displays became more important and were fitted to all twenty cars. These took the form of roller blinds, fitted within boxes suspended from the upper deck rails of the double-deckers, or mounted above the roof line of the two single-deck cars.

The extended two-road depot at St Marks included several inspection pits randomly distributed, with additional offices and other ancillary accommodation. A short siding ran at the side of the tram shed.

With the new lines now open and a promise from the company that the original lines would be relaid by June 1905, things began to settle down. The Gas Works lines were never built and it was believed the company had concluded that those living in the Lower High Street area would generally have been unable to afford to travel regularly on their cars. The Town Council appears not to have objected to their deletion from the plans despite their earlier concern over the delay in implementation. The Manchester Street/Clarence Street/High Street/Ambrose Street loop in the town centre operated as a one-way circuit; cars travelling into town did so via Ambrose Street, while those heading for the railway stations travelled along Clarence Street. The system was now therefore complete and its total route mileage was 10.22; track mileage, allowing for the double track stretches and passing loops, was 12.23. The services were operated on the following basis:

1. Lansdown Castle – MR Station – Calcutta – St James' Station – Centre – Pittville Gates – Prestbury – Southam – Cleeve Hill (every 15 minutes to Southam, with alternate cars providing a service to Cleeve Hill).
2. Lansdown Castle – MR Station – Calcutta – St James' Station – Centre – London Road – Holy Apostles – Six Ways – Copt Elm Road – Charlton Kings (every 15 minutes).
3. Centre – Cambray – Bath Road – Norwood Arms – Leckhampton (every 15 minutes).

Fifteen cars were needed to maintain these basic services, allowing a very small margin from the fleet of twenty to cover maintenance outages and the provision of duplicates; on race days for example additional cars ran to Prestbury.

Over the years there were to be frequent discussions within the council and its committees over the state of the track, the punctuality of the cars, the levels of fares and the charges for electricity. All of these were dealt with in a relatively straightforward matter and generally all went as well as might have been expected. The cars were indeed well supported, to the extent that complaints of overcrowding were raised from time to time; the council's line was that enforcement action would be taken against the company whenever they were able to obtain reliable evidence.

Passengers did not always themselves adhere to the company's rules. Reference to the company's bye-laws (see page 46 & 47) will show that the carriage of dogs was very much at the discretion of the conductor on each car. A former tram conductor recalled how on one occasion a lady boarded his car wearing an ankle-length dress. After she had travelled some distance the car suddenly accelerated and to the great embarrassment of the lady, but to the amusement of her fellow passengers, two small dogs began barking, and suddenly shot out from within the folds of her fashionable attire.

The Cheltenham system did however develop an enviable safety record; indeed at the enquiry into the 1905 extensions it was noted that, apart from the over-turning of the car before the system had been opened to the public, there had been no accidents involving any of the initial fleet. Apart from the death of a permanent way worker mentioned in the next chapter, records of only two other significant accidents have been traced. The first led to the death of a cyclist who collided with a tram outside the Bathurst Arms in London Road in August 1913. Thirty-six-year-old Mr Charles Drake was returning home to Charlton Kings on Saturday evening following visits to a number of Cheltenham ale houses; he came up behind a slow-moving butcher's cart and pulled out to overtake it – finding himself immediately in the path of a Cheltenham-bound tramcar. Mr Drake died instantly. At the inquest, a verdict of accidental death was returned, with no blame attaching to the tram driver; indeed the skill of the motormen of the Cheltenham and District Light Railway was acknowledged by the coroner.

On another occasion, of which the date is not known, a further accident occurred on the slopes of Cleeve Hill. Mr McCormick recalled in a statement made in 1920 that a motorman, operating against instructions, had attempted to take a car up the hill when snow was lying about six inches deep. After climbing a short distance, 'the car ran away with him, jumped over a fence and went into a field – but no-one was hurt, not even the driver'.

An unidentified car of the 1-8 batch is about to enter the passing loop in Cirencester Road at Charlton Kings; Pumphrey's Road is on the right. Decency boards and destination boxes are both in place, and the car appears to be in the later livery; the date is probably c.1912.

Car no.14 at Holy Apostles' church. Cirencester Road heads to the right; cars re-joined this road having first taken the left fork (London Road) to Six Ways, and then travelled via Copt Elm Road and Lyefield Road. The junction also marked the boundary between the Borough of Cheltenham and the Charlton Kings Urban District, which survived as an independent authority until 1974. The passing loop is very clearly visible in the foreground. The view dates from c.1910. In those days pedestrians could safely wander in the road; today this is a very busy junction, and has for many years been controlled by traffic lights.

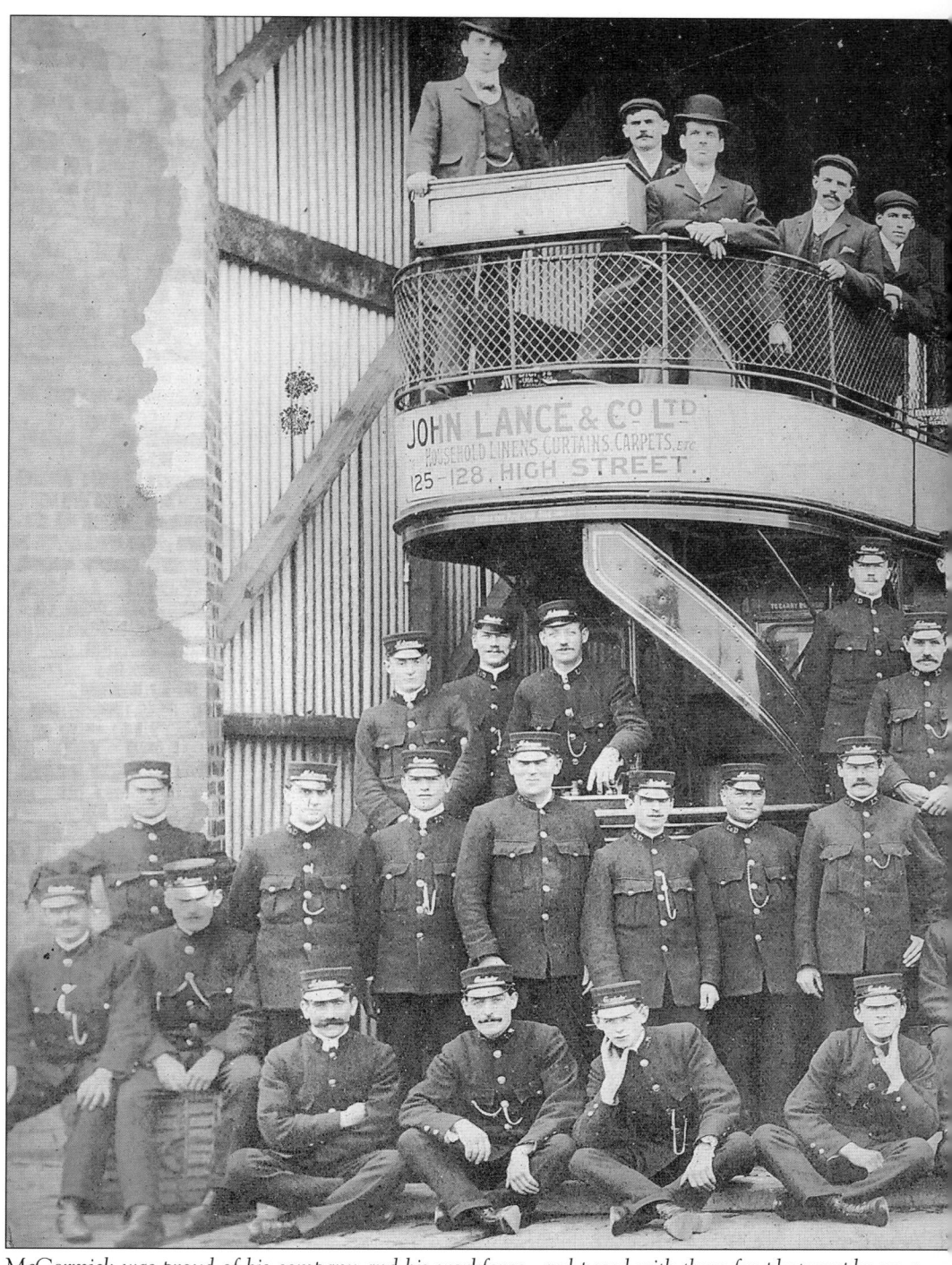

McCormick was proud of his company and his workforce, and posed with them for photographs on a number of occasions. This photograph of more than seventy of the company's staff was taken at St Mark's depot with two cars visible, that on the left is one of the 1905 cars, while that on the right is one of the earlier arrivals. Mr McCormick is seated, front centre, with his arms folded. Note the metal

cladding forming the west wall of the main depot building. The 1905 car looks new and the photograph probably dates from the year of its delivery, possibly to mark the completion of the new depot (although referred to as an extension, there are indications that the main tram shed was in fact completely rebuilt). The gentlemen on the upper decks of the cars are permanent way staff.

The first of the Renault vans, AD 2700, features in this advertisement which the company placed in the local press in 1912, when the van was new. Note that the office was originally signwritten, a little informally, in the name of Cheltenham Tramways, whereas in the view below the signwriting has been amended to the formal title of the Cheltenham & District Light Railway Co.

A surprising number of photographs of the parcels vans were taken, presumably mainly for publicity purposes. Seen with the messenger boys is the second of the 1912 Renault vans, AD 2767; the van was still going strong when this view was taken in the early 1920s. The North Street office of the Tramways Co., and the hub of the parcels operation, provides the backcloth. From the left are: Arthur Higgs, Arthur Herbert, -?-, Fred Ballinger, Bill Price, Jim Dicks, Frank Wood, Arthur Dowding and Albert Upton.

Six

The Parcels Service and Other Ancillary Vehicles

It became clear after the first few winters that the tramcars were often better equipped to climb Cleeve Hill in adverse weather conditions than any other vehicles. In part, this was as a consequence of the determination of the company, whenever snow or other obstructions threatened to disrupt operations, to send out all available employees on the first car of the day to clear the lines. With an almost total guarantee of the service running throughout the year, it quickly became standard practice for the cars to be used as a means of making deliveries on behalf of local traders to their customers in the Cleeve Hill area. Parcel boys were taken on by the company specifically for this profitable sideline. They would travel to Cleeve Hill on one of the first cars of the day, taking a small trolley with them, and spend much of the day delivering parcels including daily provisions and even newspapers. They would progressively work their way down the hill, and then travel back up on a later car, before starting the cycle over again. The parcels service quickly extended to deliveries throughout the town; for the more urban areas several delivery bicycles were acquired and more school-leavers recruited. So successful was the service that in September 1912 a 9hp Renault van took to the road. Registered AD 2700 and finished in the company's livery; this improved facility attracted even more custom and a second Renault, this time a 10hp model registered AD 2767, was placed in service three months later, apparently in a blue livery. Why a different livery was used is not clear; it may have been a conscious decision to alert the public that two different vans were now available. It has been suggested that it operated under an early form of contract hire arrangement for one of the service's main customers. The parcels service operated from an office at 3 North Street; this also served as a waiting room for passengers using the Cleeve Hill services. As will be explained in Chapter 11, the parcel service eventually formed part of a national delivery network.

Both vans survived until the early 1920s when they were replaced by McCormick's Arrol Johnson car, which had been converted at the depot by the construction of a goods compartment at the rear. A succession of vans arrived after 1926. The Arrol Johnson was not the first car to be available to the company as Mr Nevins had taken delivery of a Thomas saloon as early as June 1905; this vehicle was registered AD 525 and motor taxation records show the St Mark's depot as its registered address.

All tramway undertakings require a means of accessing the overhead wires both for routine maintenance and emergency repairs. A horse-drawn tower wagon was in use for many years until replaced in October 1924 by a petrol-driven FWD truck on which a tower had been mounted; the vehicle was registered DD 5530 and remained in use until the system had been dismantled.

Several of the trams had additional fitments to allow for a rail grinder or snow plough to be attached. There was also a four-wheel trolley for use by the permanent way staff; its general use was on the Prestbury – Cleeve Hill section where the track was laid on a ballast bed to the side of the main road. The ballast regularly needed topping up, levelling or re-packing, and when required on location the trolley was towed by one of the tramcars and left in a convenient passing loop. On one tragic occasion the truck with one of the permanent way staff on board ran away from one of the loops on the lower slopes of the hill; the worker was killed when the truck overturned.

The postmark on this card is 1912. Car no.16 makes its way towards the town centre, along the double-track section, having just passed the junction with Rodney Road (in the left foreground). The car is heading for Lansdown Castle via the Great Western and Midland stations.

Cars nos 6 and 17 are seen passing each other on the double-track section of the Charlton Kings line, just on the Cheltenham side of the Hales Road junction.

Car no.18 lays over at Leckhampton terminus. Every opportunity was taken to create advertising space. The risers of some of the stairs carried adverts, in this case even the entrance step advertises Cheltenham Ales. Ironically the main advertising space has fallen vacant. A poster in the side window draws attention to a concert by the band of His Majesty's Irish Guards. Note the fashionable moustaches sported by both the motorman and conductor.

The longitudinal seats downstairs are being demonstrated by a lady ready for a trip into Cheltenham. The conductor is upstairs, distracted by a passenger while reversing the backs of the seats on that deck. Car no.13, by this time looking a little worn, is seen in Cirencester Road outside the New Inn at which the service to Charlton Kings terminated. The entrance to Charlton Kings Station was just a hundred yards away.

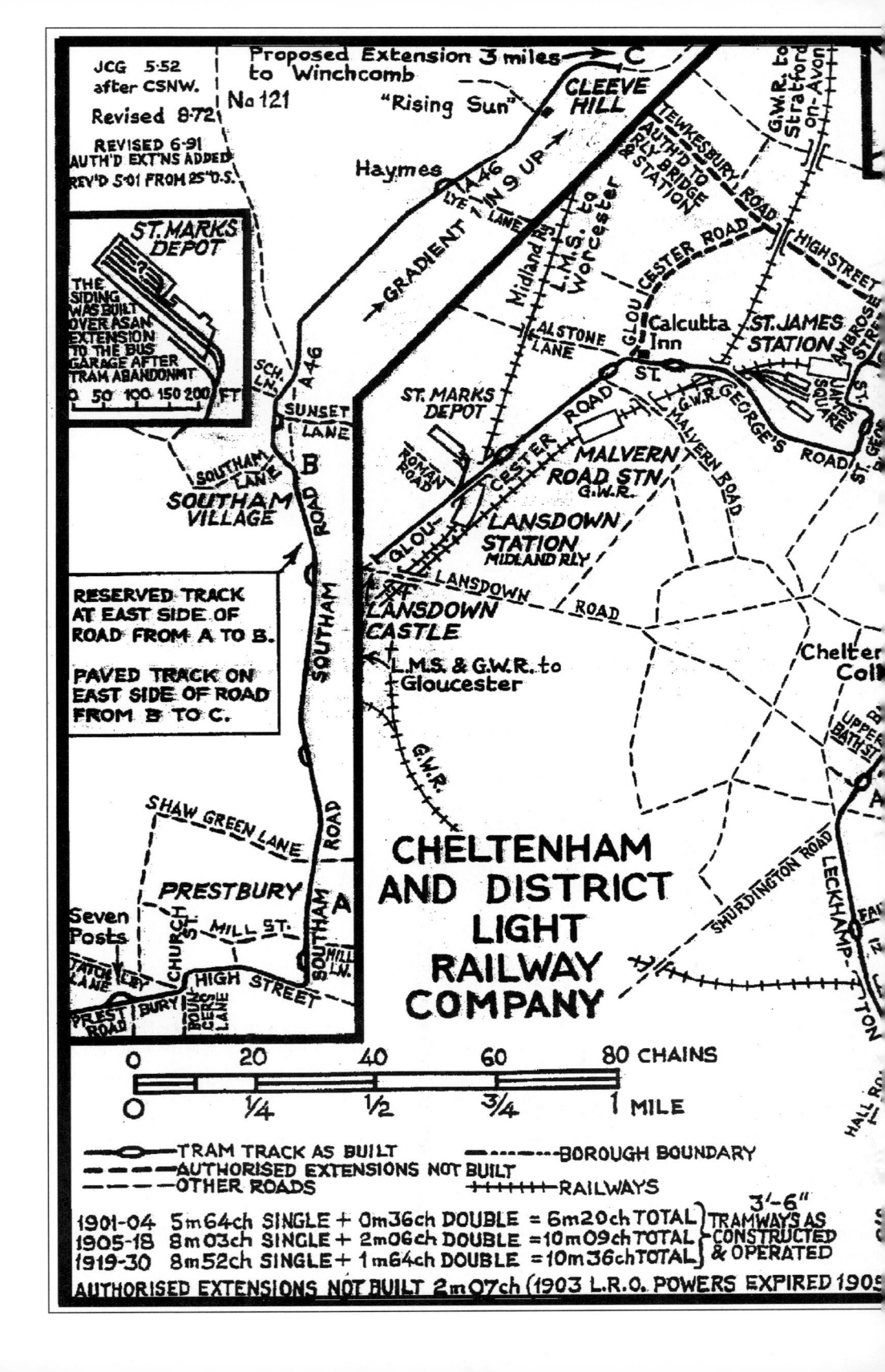

CHELTENHAM AND DISTRICT LIGHT RAILWAY COMPANY

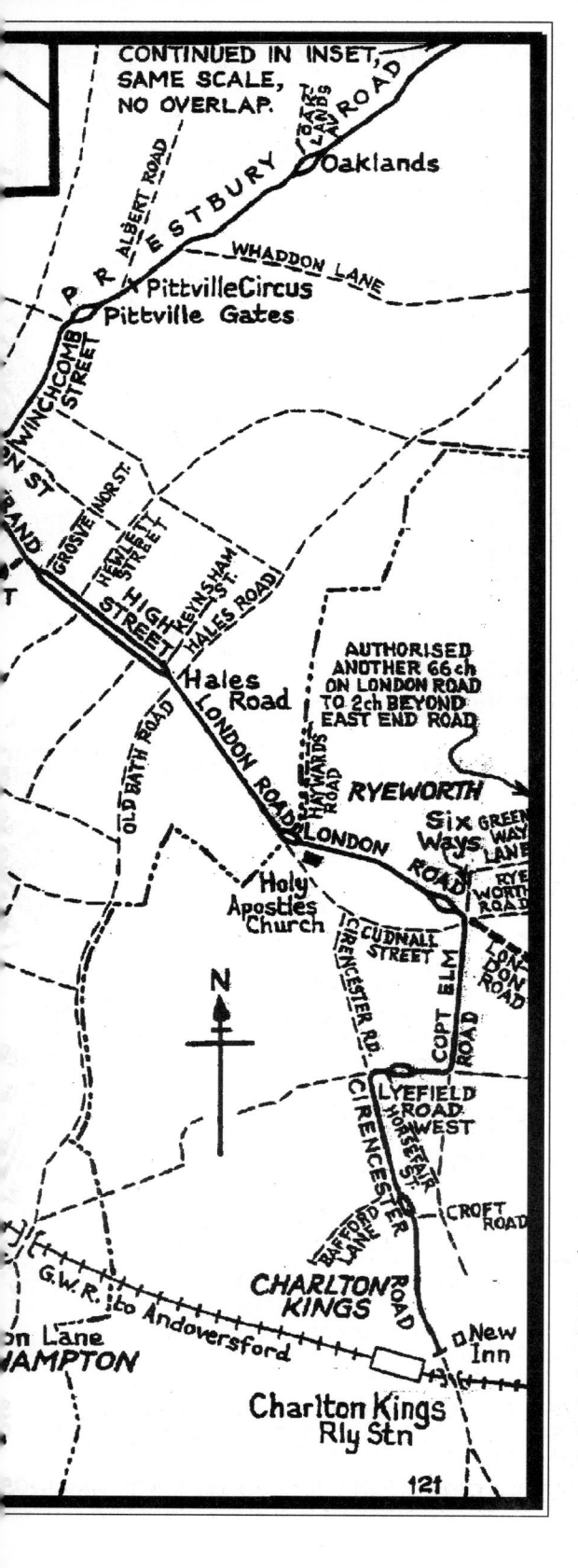

This detailed map shows the final extent of the Cheltenham tramway system; Mr John Gillham has generously re-drawn the map, which he first produced fifty years ago, to take into account further points of detail which came to light during the researches for this book. Note the reference to a proposal for a further extension in Charlton Kings; this is believed never to have been explored in any detail.

Car no.15, seemingly in as-new condition, passes Pittville Gates as it heads for Cleeve Hill. The car would not itself have run beyond Southam, passengers transferring to one of the single-deckers in that village for the trip up the hill.

By the 1920s, and possibly much earlier, the Light Railway Co. was producing very professional timetable booklets. As on the trams themselves, every available space was used to generate advertising revenue, as exemplified by this front cover.

Seven

The Second Decade of the Tramway Era

Tramway operations were at a relatively steady state as the system matured, although there were some modifications to the cars as detailed in Chapter 8. It was however other activities which contributed most of the highlights of the company's second decade of operations, including the partial motorisation of the parcels service already mentioned in Chapter 6.

In February 1911 the company applied to the Cheltenham Corporation for permission to run three motor buses to the town's racecourse for the March race meeting. Presumably the company planned to hire vehicles to operate this service, but their application was rejected.

During 1912 public pressure was mounting for buses to serve the areas of the town not within comfortable reach of the tram routes. Residents in Montpellier formally requested the Town Council to consider the introduction of a motor bus service from the Promenade to the Midland Station via Montpellier and Queens' Road. The Light Railway Co. immediately asked the council not to issue any motor bus licences from the MR station as these would be in opposition to the tramway.

Presumably prompted by the Montpellier residents, the Bristol Tramways and Carriage Co. (BTCC), which had established a base in Cheltenham just two months earlier, duly submitted an application in August of that year to run an hourly motor bus service from Westal Green via Montpellier, the Promenade and High Street to Hewlett Road. Also in August, the Light Railway Co. itself sought the grant of a licence for a service from the MR Station to the town centre. Both applications were adjourned by the council for further consideration. BTCC understandably became impatient after several months had elapsed and in January 1913 lodged an amended application, this time for the service to run from the MR Station via Westal Green to Hewlett Road. Not to be outdone by this newcomer, the Light Railway Co. renewed its own application.

The General Purposes and Watch Committee (GPWC), who dealt with such applications, established a sub-committee to consider the issues involved. The sub-committee reported promptly, and at the GPWC meeting on 18 February it was agreed that a licence would be granted to the Light Railway Co. The committee agreed that the latter could ill afford any abstraction of its tramway custom; its decision took into account the significant contribution the company made to the town's coffers through rates payable on its premises (£400 per annum) and the electricity it purchased (£4,000 each year). The motor bus service would operate hourly and approval was conditional upon it being introduced within three months. The fares to be applied were determined to be as follows:

MR Station – Montpellier: 1d
Montpellier – Royal Hotel: 1d
High Street – Cemetery: 1d

It may have been the specification of a maximum three-month start-up period which led to the service being introduced using a hired Commer WP fourteen-seater charabanc, seemingly on short-term loan from the manufacturer. Even with this arrangement, the launch of the service did not fall quite within the three-month deadline; operations eventually began on 31 May. Although only on loan, the vehicle carried the Light Railway Co.'s red livery and their name in full. It seated fourteen passengers and was entirely open to the elements; it was registered BM 26x0 (the third digit being unclear on the only photograph available). The council granted a driver's licence to Mr W.G. Rich, who quoted an address in Lavender Hill, London SW. It may therefore be reasonably assumed that Mr Rich had arrived with the charabanc, possibly with the intention that he would impart his driving skills to some local men during his visit to Gloucestershire. The charabanc operated in the town for only a few weeks as the more permanent vehicle that the company had been awaiting duly arrived the following month. This again was a Commer, but a larger WP2 with fully enclosed single-deck bodywork seating twenty-four. Five of the company's own staff were now licensed to drive the vehicle: Messrs. J.H. Spawton, H.J. Curtis, H.B. Turner, A.H. Walker and F. Drinkwater.

As far as may be ascertained, the service operated as envisaged for about a year but the vehicle, like so many others of its generation, was then requisitioned for military service. An understanding public appears not to have raised any objections to the loss of their service. More surprisingly however, Cheltenham was not again to be provided with an urban bus service until 1924.

To digress a little, the very first proposals to run motor bus services in Cheltenham had been made as early as 1908. In that year Mr H.E. Steel, a local garage proprietor, lodged an application for a licence to run a ten-seater charabanc on a service from the Promenade to the MR Station via Montpellier, and the London Electrobus Company planned to operate an electric bus in the town. However, the GPWC rejected both applications and no appeals were made. Another motor bus service was, though, running in the town, almost certainly before the outbreak of the First World War; in this case it was not for use by the general public. The service was sponsored by a consortium of local hotels and the small bus was provided by BTCC; it shuttled between the hotels and the Midland Station at which it connected with all main trains. This small bus of Lacre manufacture was permitted only to carry hotel guests. BTCC went on to introduce a motor bus service from Cheltenham to Tewkesbury on 6 November 1915 and shortly afterwards sought approval from the Town Council for additional stopping places in both the High Street and Tewkesbury Road. An objection was received from the Light Railway Co. and upheld by the council, even though no

Cars were occasionally made available for private parties, even during the war years. Here 1902 car no.12 carries a good load of youngsters from The Elms Children's Home in the town. Mr Agg Gardner, one time mayor of Cheltenham and for many years the local MP, was treating them to a day out on Cleeve Hill in August 1915. (Gloucestershire Echo)

tramways passed further west than the Ambrose Street/High Street junction. Logic however prevailed and the application was granted on appeal the following month. Over the next few years BTCC and a number of other operators, large and small, began regular motor bus services into Cheltenham from many surrounding towns and villages.

Not only did 1914 see the outbreak of war, but it also saw the sale of the Cheltenham District Light Railway Co. Mr Nevins had decided to dispose of his Cheltenham asset and a ready buyer was found in the form of Balfour Beatty and Co. Ltd, a holding company that already controlled tramways in a number of towns. The Cheltenham operation was put under the control of one of its subsidiaries, the Midland Counties Electrical Supply Co. The Cheltenham Co. was reformed under its original name and Henry McCormick remained in control, now in the roles of Director and General Manager. The company was to remain with Balfour Beatty for the next quarter of a century.

Balfour Beatty was at that time still a relatively new group, having been formed in 1909. A number of electrical power and transport companies were to be acquired (and sold) over the following decades, covering many areas of both England and Scotland. Within thirty miles of Cheltenham the group controlled the Leamington and Warwick tramway system, and later acquired the Stratford Blue bus company. Many of the acquired operations, like that in Cheltenham, were managed by intermediate subsidiary companies.

Not only did the war deprive the town of its bus service but it also affected the tram services in a number of ways, not least through the shortage of manpower. For the first time ladies were recruited as conductresses, albeit on a temporary basis, both to replace directly conscripted conductors, and also to fill in behind those conductors who in turn had suddenly found themselves re-trained as drivers. An amusing tale was told by one of these ladies. Whenever she was conducting on the Charlton Kings route a gentleman admirer, who lived in Copt Elm Road and was a keen gardener, made sure he would always be tending his front garden whenever her car was due to pass. On each occasion, to her great embarrassment, he would toss a red rose onto the platform of the car.

Such distractions apart, times were hard and austerity measures resulted in a number of the trams themselves appearing in an all-over grey livery while all destination boxes were removed and replaced by slip-boards placed at the foot of the central side windows. Small destination boards were also introduced, to be hung beneath the cars' canopies.

Car no.19 makes the sharp turn from High Street into Cambray Place en route for Leckhampton. It was at this point that the Leckhampton and Charlton Kings lines diverged. The car looks in very good shape and the photograph was probably taken soon after it was delivered in 1905.

This Commer charabanc was the town's first bus. It was on loan from the manufacturer for only a brief period in the spring of 1913, while the Light Railway Co. awaited delivery of the motor bus they had ordered for the introduction of a new service from the Midland Station to Harp Hill via Montpellier and the town centre. By borrowing this charabanc the company was able to introduce the service within, or rather almost within(!), the deadline which they had been given by the Cheltenham Corporation as a condition of a licence for the service being granted. The vehicle was registered BM 26x0, the third digit being unclear on this, the only known photograph, taken in Queen's Road, opposite the Midland Station. The driver is in civilian dress; we may never know whether he was a new recruit, still awaiting an issue of uniform, or the Commer employee who had accompanied the vehicle.

The company's own bus, another Commer, was ready just a few weeks later. The vehicle seated twenty-four and is seen in this posed shot outside the manager's office at the depot at St Mark's, probably when newly delivered. Like so many vehicles of its time, the Commer was impressed for military service during First World War, and the bus service was suspended. Note that the conductor is the same gentleman as in the previous view. It carried the same livery as the trams.

PUBLIC NOTICE

COMMENCING JUNE 2ND 1913

A

MOTOR 'BUS SERVICE

Will be Run by the

CHELTENHAM AND DISTRICT LIGHT RAILWAY COMPANY

From the **MIDLAND STATION** via **THE PROMENADE** and **HIGH STREET** to the Foot of **HARP HILL** at 10.20 a.m. and every 40 minutes thereafter to 8.20 p.m., and from the Foot of **HARP HILL** to the **MIDLAND STATION** at 10.40 a.m. and every 40 minutes to 8.40 p.m.

STAGES AND FARES

Midland Station and Montpellier Gates	1d
Montpellier Gates and Saxby's Cambray Pharmacy	1d
Saxby's Cambray Pharmacy and Foot of Harp Hill	1d
Midland Station and Saxby's Cambray Pharmacy	2d
Montpellier Gates and Foot of Harp Hill	2d
Midland Station and Foot of Harp Hill	3d

The company placed this Public Notice in the local press to announce the launch of its first motor bus service in June 1913.

An interesting comparison of the frontal appearances of the 1905 and 1921 cars is provided by no.20 obligingly standing alongside no.22 in the passing loop just a hundred yards from the LMS Station on Gloucester Road. The photograph is thought to date from the early 1920s; the destination box has not been restored to the 1905 car, and the replacement indicator board introduced during the war years is still suspended from its canopy.

Car no.20, numerically the last of the 1905 batch, is seen on its own in this view, turning into the passing loop in Lyefield Road West. No passengers are visible, the car looks pristine and the crew appear to have been expecting the photographer. This may therefore have been a pre-arranged publicity shot.

Eight

The 1920s

Fares had always been the subject of much debate both in the council chamber and more generally among members of the public, for whom the tramways were often the only realistic form of local transport. In October 1920 the company made a detailed submission to the Tramways Charges Advisory Committee. The company was anxious that the committee should consider whether an Order might be issued increasing the maximum charges for the conveyance of both passengers and goods. The committee had been set up under the Tramways (Temporary Increase of Charges) Act 1920, probably as a result of concerns expressed by the managers of many undertakings over their inability to invest in replacement cars and infrastructure following the difficult years of the First World War. It reported to the Minister of Transport. A public enquiry was held in London on 14 December to consider the situation in Cheltenham. The committee recommended that an Order be issued authorising the following basis for the calculation of the company's fares:

   i)   2d per mile, or part mile, for ordinary passengers.
   ii) For workmen, a return fare at the rate of an ordinary single fare.
   iii) For goods and parcels, an increase of 100% over the fares set out in the original 1900 Order, or alternatively a 50% increase for their carriage with reasonable charges for any additional handling requirements.

However, the situation was terribly complex. Any new Order issued would over-ride any agreements made between the company and the Cheltenham Corporation (in line with the requirements of the original 1900 Order). Several months prior to this hearing the Minister of Transport had agreed to some of the company's demands for fare increases, but as a temporary measure only until this hearing by the committee had probed the situation in more detail. The company had however not implemented those provisional agreements until it had received the Cheltenham Corporation's reluctant blessing. At the end of this hearing, the committee recommended that any new Order should respect the level of fares previously agreed, and that the company could only increase them further with the specific agreement of the Minister of Transport. While they acknowledged the important role of the Cheltenham Corporation, they were unable to delegate any of the Minister's powers in this matter to the local authority. The hearing in London was attended by, among others, Cheltenham's Town Clerk, the assistant Clerk to the Cheltenham Rural District Council, a representative of the Gloucestershire County Council, and three company officials.

The detailed papers submitted to the committee contained many interesting snippets of information about the company's operations at that time; among them were the following:

i)   Once the increased fares had been introduced, the estimated annual takings would be £34,700 – leaving an operating surplus of only £5,130 to meet interest payments, tax demands, dividends and items of capital expenditure.

ii)   The company was under statutory obligation to run special early cars for workmen, but argued that there was no demand for such operations in the town; the availability of workmen's fares on ordinary services was seen as a realistic compromise.

iii)   Children were carried at half-fares only when travelling to school.

iv)   The actual route length was 10 miles 3 furlongs 4.73 chains, with the lines being laid in the territories of no fewer than four local authorities:
5 miles 5 furlongs 1.95 chains: Borough of Cheltenham.
1 mile 5 furlongs 8.64 chains: Cheltenham Rural District Council.
1 mile 2 furlongs 8.9 chains: Charlton Kings Urban District Council.
1 mile 5 furlongs 3.23 chains: Winchcombe Rural District Council.
Of the total mileage, 8 miles 5 furlongs was single track, and 1 mile 6.5 furlongs was double-track.

v)   Maximum charges for parcels ranged from 3d for those up to 7lbs, to 9d for those between 28lbs and 56lbs.

vi)   The capital of the company was £120,000 made up of £19,000 in preference shares, £71,000 in ordinary shares and £30,000 debenture stock.

vii)   The following comparisons were drawn between 1913 and 1920:

	1913	1920
Operating margin:	£6,388	£2,408
Receipts per car mile:	6.61d	18.31d
Expenses per car mile:	4.42d	16.87d
Total car mileage*:	701,123	403,920
Ordinary passenger journeys:	2,512,944	3,333,388
Working week for crews:	57 hours	48 hours

* A reduction of 208,000 miles occurred between 1915 and 1916; the figures for 1918, 1919 and 1920 were all only marginally in excess of 400, 000.

viii)   The first car of the day ran at 7.15 a.m.

ix)   Service frequencies in 1920 were as follows:

Lansdown Castle – North Street: 7½min
North Street – Leckhampton: 12min/10min (Saturdays)
North Street – Southam: 30min (winter)/15min (summer)
North Street – Cleeve Hill: hourly (winter)/15 min (high summer)

x)   The delivery of new cars now on order would enable the company to maintain a fleet of twenty operational cars i.e. the new arrivals would displace a similar number of older cars.

Three new cars, numbered 21-23, did indeed arrive in 1921 having been built by English Electric on Peckham trucks. At the December 1920 fares hearing in London, detailed above, the company had stated that four new cars were on order, at a cost of £2,500 each; it is understood that the fourth car was diverted elsewhere without ever arriving in Cheltenham. Sixteen years had elapsed since the last cars had been delivered and this was reflected in the much more modern appearance of these new cars. Two of the main differences were the fitting of fully enclosed vestibules – for the first time giving the motormen protection from the elements – and the arrangement of the staircases which, unlike the earlier cars, were left-ascending. These double-deckers were however still of open-top design; they seated twenty-three inside and twenty-nine on top. Their regular deployment was on the Cleeve Hill route as the inclusion of electromagnetic track brakes in their build specification had removed the need for any further braking modifications for safe operation on the gradient. Unlike all earlier cars the lower saloons were fitted with reversible transverse seats of the same pattern as those used on the upper deck.

As noted above these were not regarded as additional cars, but were seen as replacements for some of the original fleet, which, after twenty years of service, had reached the end of their useful lives. The picture had become somewhat blurred through rebuilding and re-numbering of the cars. Some rebuilding had even taken place during the war years but is thought not to have changed the identities or basic features of any of the cars, other than for the repositioning of the side-mounted trolley masts on the original cars to a central position. As the original red upholstery on the lower deck seats of nos 1-12 wore out, it was replaced by the cane-straw variety as fitted from new on the later cars. During the early 1920s however, during a refurbishment of single-decker no.9, the upper-deck fitments of no.12 were grafted on, the latter then becoming a single-decker. The cars were out of use for some time during their refurbishment and to maintain a single-deck fleet strength of two, no.2 temporarily ran as a single-decker. Following the withdrawal of the other original single-decker, no.10, no.3 joined no.12 as a second single-deck conversion. Such conversions were relatively straightforward as most upper deck fitments simply unbolted. The stairs too could easily be removed.

A number of cars had their Peckham trucks replaced with those of Brill manufacture while most of the original ten double-deckers (1-8, 11 and 12) lost their slipper brakes thus ensuring that they did not again venture beyond Southam when operating on the Cleeve Hill route.

During the second half of the decade, three cars were extensively rebuilt; they received enclosed vestibules and thereafter much more closely resembled nos 21-23. The rebuilds were nos 14, 16 and 19 of the 1905 batch; although no.16 retained its number, for some reason nos 14 and 19 were re-numbered 10 and 1 respectively, those numbers having become vacant through scrapping.

Also acquired as replacements for earlier cars were two second-hand vehicles, which predictably took numbers 24 and 25; these had previously served in nearby Worcester where they had been numbered 17 and 16 respectively. These arrived in the town in 1928, following abandonment of the Worcester system. They were mounted on Brill trucks and were semi-vestibuled, but to a rather more rounded design than on 21–23.

Destination boxes with roller blinds reappeared on all cars in the early 1920s; the side-mounted slip boards were retained but were now displayed inside the windows rather than on the outside of the cars.

After a surprisingly long gap, particularly as many other buses were by this time operating into the town, local bus services re-appeared in 1924, albeit initially covering only one route. The Light Railway Co. had successfully applied to the GPWC in November 1923 for licences for three motor buses to operate from St Mark's to the Cemetery via Tennyson Road, Gloucester Road, Midland Station, Queen's Road, Westal Green, Montpellier, High Street and Hewlett Road. Three Guy single-deck buses duly arrived in the town at the end of the following February and were put into service early in March. After just a few weeks the council agreed that alternate afternoon journeys would divert at Westal Green to run via Tivoli and Park Place, re-joining the original route at Montpellier; an hourly frequency was maintained on each route.

A further successful application was made in April 1925 for an hourly service from the Centre to Sandy Lane via Suffolk Square, Thirlestaine Road and Old Bath Road. Only one month later, the service was extended beyond the Centre to terminate at the bridge carrying Tewkesbury Road over the LMS railway line. The following December a further application was made for the service to run from the Centre to Cheltenham racecourse. The Tewkesbury Road service appears to have been abandoned at that time. Interestingly this service was operated on a one-man basis, with the driver also taking the fares, a practice that died out in 1939, only to reappear in the late 1960s. The introduction of the initial Sandy Lane service had resulted in all three buses being rostered for duty every day and to provide some backup a licence for a fourth bus was obtained in October 1925.

The three original buses were registered DD 3955-3957 and were presumably numbered 1-3, but in uncertain order; it is only known that DD 3955 was numbered 3. They were Guy BBs and carried thirty-seat single-deck bodies built by Strachan and Brown. The fourth bus, another BB and numbered 4, was registered DD 8170; for this vehicle Strachan and Brown fitted a twenty-eight-seat body, two seats having been lost through the fitting of a second door.

For several days in November 1921 tram services had been halted following a walk-out by staff in protest at a lengthening of their hours and a reduction in their pay. The year had seen a general increase in tension in the field of labour relations and the miners' strike in South Wales had perhaps encouraged others to take more localised action with the hope of a betterment in their working conditions. The pay rates of Cheltenham's tram crews just a few years earlier are known to have been as follows:

Conductors: $3\frac{1}{2}$d per hour
Drivers: 5d per hour
Cleeve Hill drivers: $5\frac{1}{2}$d per hour (i.e. the equivalent of just under 2p per hour)

The manager was quick to demonstrate that he was in control and immediately set about the recruitment of replacement staff. During the training of one of the novices as a motorman, car no.16 suffered minor damage in a collision, causing some embarrassment as a press photographer was on hand at the time!

It was however the General Strike of 1926 which caused more disruption. This strike of course affected most towns and cities throughout the country. A number of local tram and bus crews withdrew their labour in support of what they believed to be a just cause. The company's reaction was swift and firm. The *Gloucestershire Echo* reported as follows on 13 May 1926, under the heading of 'Tramway impasse: Manager wants non-unionists only':

The position with reference to the Cheltenham District Light Railway, a large number of whose motormen, conductors and other employees joined in the general strike at the orders of the TUC, is quite different from that with the big railways. The company having been deserted by its union men is apparently going to endeavour to run their works with non-unionists. On Wednesday the following notice was posted at the works and the tramway office in North Street:

"Notice from H J McCormick to all who dismissed themselves from work: Kindly turn in all uniforms and all property of the company within the next 12 hours and collect your insurance cards. Applications for re-employment will be considered only from non-union men."

Mr McCormick told the Echo that he had got a nice lot of young fellows whom he was going to start training for the work required of them.

The mood soon softened a little and some of those who had heeded the call of the TUC were re-employed but only once they had left their union and agreed to work longer hours for their previous money!

The mid-1920s saw further protracted debate over tram fares, with a dispute in 1924 finally being heard by the Board of Trade at a meeting convened in London. As ever, the Cheltenham Corporation and the company eventually reached an amicable agreement and in 1927 the fares were further reviewed and both parties agreed to the following:

North Street to Pittville Gates: 1d
LMS Station to St George's Place: 2d
LMS Station to North Street: 2½d
North Street to Hewlett Road: 1d
Hewlett Road to Holy Apostles: 1½d
Cambray to Thirlestaine Road: 1d
Thirlestaine Road to Norwood Arms: 1d
Norwood Arms to Hall Road: 1d
Hall Road to Foot of Leckhampton Hill: 1d
Thirlestaine Road to Hall Road: 1½d

In April 1927 permission was given for some localised re-routing of alternate motor bus journeys around St Mark's estate in order to serve better some new areas of housing. Later that year the local constabulary was becoming concerned about traffic congestion in the town and instructed that all buses from St Mark's and Sandy Lane must approach the town centre via the Gordon Lamp, Montpellier Street, Royal Well Lane, Clarence Parade, and Clarence Street. The stops in the Promenade had also to be relocated and were now placed nearer to the fountain, and no longer near County Court Road.

Similar concerns over traffic congestion had also affected some tramway operations in the central area. Cars on the Cleeve Hill service now terminated at the centre rather than proceeding to the LMS station; the latter area was of course still served by Charlton Kings cars, and also by some of the new bus services. Cars from Leckhampton now continued to St James' station, rather than reversing in the centre. Note that the station at Lansdown was by this time properly referred to as the LMS Station, the former Midland Railway having become a constituent of the London, Midland and Scottish Railway at the time of the 1923 Grouping.

In March 1928 the company made another successful licence application for three extra motor buses. These were required to operate on a new route from Pilford via Pilley Bridge, Old Bath Road, High Street, the Gas Works and the LMS Station to St Mark's, and on an extension of the Cemetery service to Cleeve Hill. This development led to the arrival of another Guy, albeit second-hand, and the loan of two Tilling-Stevens. The Guy was another model B; it was registered RA 4210 and took fleet no.5. It had been new to a small operator by the name of Hayton in Mansfield, but became surplus to requirements when Hayton was bought out by Midland General, another member of the Balfour Beatty group and a new home was therefore sought within the group.

The two loaned vehicles also came from the Midland General company. They were Tilling Stevens B10Bs with thirty-two-seat Strachan and Brown bodies. The pair, registered RA 3958/9, are thought to have arrived in Cheltenham in February 1928 but were back home in Nottinghamshire by the start of 1929. It would appear that the new routes authorised in 1928 were short-lived, and the Cleeve Hill extension may in fact not have materialised. The April 1929 timetable showed an hourly service being operated between the Racecourse and Sandy Lane, a similar frequency on the Pilford-St Mark's service, but with a thirty minute headway on the St Mark's-Cemetery route. There was no Sunday service to Sandy Lane, but on the other two services Sunday afternoon operation was as on weekdays. The weekday afternoon vehicle requirement stood at four vehicles. While there had been some fairly regular changes to the routes as these early bus services bedded down, some rather bigger changes were however by then on the horizon, as will be explained in subsequent Chapters.

Another assembly of the Light Railway Co.'s staff, this time in 1923. St Mark's depot is looking rather more mature than in the view on pages 50 and 51. Once again, Mr McCormick is sitting in the front centre, this time somewhat older, and wearing a bowler hat; his son is sitting in front of him, wearing a mortar board. Note how the uniforms have changed since the earlier photograph was taken. Neither of the cars had at this time received the new destination boxes, which were gradually re-introduced as the 1920s wore on. The following members of staff have been identified:

Front row (on floor) – *Third left: Fred (Nobby) Ballinger. Fourth right: Frank Wood. Second row (seated) – Fourth left: Bill Flook. Fifth left: Harry Hales. 3rd right (bowler hat): Ossie Wildsmith. Third row (standing) – Fourth left: Bert (Matey) Turner. Fifth right: Archie King. Sixth right: Walter Wells. Ninth right: Bill Slatter. Back double row – Third left: Bert Cleevely. Eighth left: Fred Simpson. Tall man in centre: Bill Greengrass. Second right: Sid Ireland. Third right: Arthur Higgs. Fourth right: Percy Spawton. Eleventh right: Fred Davis.*

Three new cars arrived in 1921, the first for sixteen years; they were very different to the earlier cars, the more obvious improvements being the fully enclosed vestibules, the provision of transverse seating in the lower saloons, and left-ascending stairs. These English Electric cars were to serve the town for only nine years; the system was to cease operation at the end of 1930. Car no.22 is seen above on the passing loop in North Street, outside the Globe Inn. Compare the view with that on page 32 of no.2 taken at the same spot some twenty years earlier. The parcels on the sack truck are standing outside the Tramways office. Below, no.23, on arrival in the town centre from Charlton Kings, has just turned from the High Street into Clarence Street and is heading for the railway stations. In the background is the new store for E.L. Ward with its date of completion, 1923, clearly visible. (Both: A D Packer (O J Morris))

In order to replace more ageing cars, two second-hand purchases were made in 1928 from the Worcester Corporation system, which was then being abandoned. The cars had previously operated in their native town as nos 16 and 17; they became 25 and 24 respectively on arrival in Cheltenham. They had been built by the Midland Counties Co. in 1921 and had semi-enclosed vestibules. Above, no.24 is seen emerging from St Mark's depot; just visible alongside is rebuilt car no.16. This is one of three cars so treated in the early 1920s; unlike the other two, no.16 kept its original number. In their new form the vestibules were enclosed and the completed vehicles closely resembled nos 21-23. Their staircases were replaced and were now left ascending; they were however readily distinguishable from the later cars by retaining their three window layout. In the view below, no.25 also stands in the depot, possibly immediately after tramway operations had ceased. The left ascending stairs and the company bye-laws displayed on the bulkhead may be clearly seen through the unglazed section of the vestibule. Billie Dove was appearing in Careers at the local Opera House. (Omnibus Society (C F Klapper))

Lansdown	7 38	7 53	..	..	..	9 7	..	..
Midland Station	7 41	7 56	..	..	..	9 10	..	..
Calcutta	7 45	8 0	..	..	..	9 15	..	..
St. George's Place	7 49	8 4	..	..	..	9 19	..	..
North Street	7 52	8 7	8 30	8 52	9 15	9 22	9 38	9 53
Hales Road	7 59	8 14	8 36	9 0	9 20	9 30	9 45	10 0
Holy Apostles	8 0	8 16	8 38	9 2	9 23	9 32	9 47	10 2
Lyefield Road	8 5	8 21	8 41	9 7	9 25	9 38	9 53	10 8
Charlton Kings	8 10	8 27	8 47	9 12	9 31	9 44	10 0	10 14

Lansdown	1 23	1 38	1 53	2 8	2 23	2 38	2 53	3 8
Midland Station	1 26	1 41	1 56	2 11	2 26	2 41	2 56	3 11
Calcutta	1 30	1 45	2 0	2 15	2 30	2 45	3 0	3 15
St. George's Place	1 34	1 49	2 4	2 19	2 34	2 49	3 4	3 19
North Street	1 38	1 53	2 8	2 23	2 38	2 53	3 8	3 23
Hales Road	1 45	2 0	2 15	2 30	2 45	3 0	3 15	3 30
Holy Apostles	1 47	2 2	2 17	2 32	2 47	3 2	3 17	3 32
Lyefield Road	1 53	2 8	2 23	2 38	2 53	3 8	3 23	3 38
Charlton Kings	2 0	2 15	2 30	2 45	3 0	3 15	3 30	3 45

Lansdown	6 53	7 8	7 23	7 38	7 53	..	..	..
Midland Station	6 56	7 11	7 26	7 41	7 56	..	..	..
Calcutta	7 0	7 15	7 30	7 45	8 0	..	..	..
St. George's Place	7 4	7 19	7 34	7 49	8 4	..	..	..
North Street	7 8	7 23	7 38	7 53	8 8	8 15	8 30	8 45
Hales Road	7 15	7 30	7 45	8 0	8 15	8 22	8 38	8 52
Holy Apostles	7 17	7 32	7 47	8 2	8 17	8 24	8 40	8 55
Lyefield Road	7 23	7 38	7 53	8 8	8 23	8 30	8 45	9 0
Charlton Kings	7 30	7 45	7 57	8 12	8 27	8 35	8 50	9 5

1023	1038	1053	11 8	1123	1138	1153	12 8	1223	1238	1253	1 8
1026	1041	1056	1111	1126	1141	1156	1211	1226	1241	1256	1 11
1030	1045	11 0	1115	1130	1145	12 0	1215	1230	1245	1 0	1 15
1034	1049	11 4	1119	1134	1149	12 4	1219	1234	1249	1 4	1 19
1038	1053	11 8	1123	1138	1153	12 8	1223	1238	1253	1 8	1 23
1045	11 0	1115	1130	1145	12 0	1215	1230	1245	1 0	1 15	1 30
1047	11 2	1117	1132	1147	12 2	1217	1232	1247	1 2	1 17	1 32
1053	11 8	1123	1138	1153	12 8	1223	1238	1253	1 8	1 23	1 38
11 0	1115	1130	1145	12 0	1215	1230	1245	1 0	1 15	1 30	1 45

3 53	4 8	4 23	4 38	4 53	5 8	5 23	5 38	5 53	6 8	6 23	6 38
3 56	4 11	4 26	4 41	4 56	5 11	5 26	5 41	5 56	6 11	6 26	6 41
4 0	4 15	4 30	4 45	5 0	5 15	5 30	5 45	6 0	6 15	6 30	6 45
4 4	4 19	4 34	4 49	5 4	5 19	5 34	5 49	6 4	6 19	6 34	6 49
4 8	4 23	4 38	4 53	5 8	5 23	5 38	5 53	6 8	6 23	6 38	6 53
4 15	4 30	4 45	5 0	5 15	5 30	5 45	6 0	6 15	6 30	6 45	7 0
4 17	4 32	4 47	5 2	5 17	5 32	5 47	6 2	6 17	6 32	6 47	7 2
4 23	4 38	4 53	5 8	5 23	5 38	5 53	6 8	6 23	6 38	6 53	7 8
4 30	4 45	5 0	5 15	5 30	5 45	6 0	6 15	6 30	6 45	7 0	7 15

Saturday Service.—Continued to **10** o'clock from North Street.

Theatre Car Each Evening.

Sunday Service.—From North Street **2.15** until **9.0**.

A 1920s timetable for the Lansdown-Charlton Kings tram service.

For nine years following the conscription of the 1913 Commer motor bus, the town had no urban bus services. Bus services were however re-introduced in 1924 when three Guy BB saloons were delivered. They had been acquired for a new service running from St Mark's to Harp Hill. The Guys were registered DD 3955 – 3957 and carried thirty-seat bodies by Strachan and Brown. No.3 (DD 3955) is seen here when new. In the side windows are the destination boards, which read St Mark's, Harp Hill and Cemetery. Alongside are Driver Jim Fletcher and Conductor Frank Wood. The same pair is seen below with the same vehicle, but probably on another occasion. (Frank Wood)

Marks — MOTOR BUS — SERVICE. — Cemetery

Brooklyn and Tennyson Roads	...	10 0	11 0	12 0	12 30	1 0	1 30	2 0	
Railway Station	9 40	10 5	11 5	12 5	12 35	1 5	1 35	2 5	
Hotel	9 42	10 8	11 8	12 8	12 38	1 8	1 38	2 8	
					12 41		1 41	—	
Rotunda	9 45	10 11	11 11	12 11	12 44	1 11	1 44	2 11	
Post Office	9 50	10 15	11 15	12 15	12 48	1 15	1 48	2 15	
St & Hewlett Street	—	10 19	11 19	12 19	12 51	1 19	1 51	2 19	
Road	—	10 21	11 21	12 21	12 53	1 21	1 53	2 21	
ng's Rd. & Hale's Rd.	—	10 23	11 23	12 23	12 55	1 23	1 55	2 23	
	—	10 24	11 24	12 24	12 56	1 24	1 56	2 24	
arrive	—	10 28	11 28	12 28	12 59	1 28	1 59	2 28	

depart	10 30	11 30	12 30	1 0	1 30	2 0	2 30	3 0	
	10 37	11 37	12 37	1 7	1 37	2 7	2 37	3 7	
ng's Rd. & Hale's Rd.	10 38	11 38	12 38	1 8	1 38	2 8	2 38	3 8	
Road	10 40	11 40	12 40	1 10	1 40	2 10	2 40	3 10	
St & Hewlett Street	10 42	11 42	12 42	1 12	1 42	2 12	2 42	3 12	
Post Office	10 45	11 45	12 45	1 15	1 45	2 15	2 45	3 15	
Rotunda	10 49	11 49	12 49	1 18	1 49	2 18	2 49	3 18	
	—	—	—	1 21	—	2 21	—	3 21	
Hotel	10 51	11 51	12 51	1 23	1 51	2 23	2 51	3 23	
Railway Station	10 54	11 54	12 54	1 26	1 54	2 26	2 54	3 26	
Brooklyn and Tennyson Roads	10 59	11 59	12 59	1 30	1 59	2 30	2 59	3 30	

	2 30	3 0	3 30	4 0	4 30	5 0	5 30	6 0	6 30
	2 35	3 5	3 35	4 5	4 35	5 5	5 35	6 5	6 35
	2 38	3 8	3 38	4 8	4 38	5 8	5 38	6 8	6 38
	2 41	—	3 41	—	4 41	—	5 41	—	6 41
	2 44	3 11	3 44	4 11	4 44	5 11	5 44	6 11	6 44
	2 48	3 15	3 48	4 15	4 48	5 15	5 48	6 15	6 48
	2 51	3 19	3 51	4 19	4 51	5 19	5 51	6 19	6 51
	2 53	3 21	3 53	4 21	4 53	5 21	5 53	6 21	6 53
	2 55	3 23	3 55	4 23	4 55	5 23	5 55	6 23	6 55
	2 56	3 24	3 56	4 24	4 56	5 24	5 56	6 24	6 56
	2 59	3 28	3 59	4 28	4 59	5 28	5 59	6 28	6 59

	3 30	4 0	4 30	5 0	5 30	6 0	6 30	7 0	
	3 37	4 7	4 37	5 7	5 37	6 7	6 37	7 7	
	3 38	4 8	4 38	5 8	5 38	6 8	6 38	7 8	
	3 40	4 10	4 40	5 10	5 40	6 10	6 40	7 10	
	3 42	4 12	4 42	5 12	5 42	6 12	6 42	7 12	
	3 45	4 15	4 45	5 15	5 45	6 15	6 45	7 15	
	3 49	4 18	4 49	5 18	5 49	6 18	6 49	7 18	
	—	4 21	—	5 21	—	6 21	—	7 21	
	3 51	4 23	4 51	5 23	5 51	6 23	6 51	7 23	
	3 54	4 26	4 54	5 26	5 54	6 26	6 54	7 26	
	3 59	4 30	4 59	5 30	5 59	6 30	6 59	7 30	

FARES

n Brooklyn and Tennyson Roads and L.M.S. Station
Station and Lansdown Hotel.
wn Hotel and Montpellier Rotunda.
llier Rotunda and Colonnade
de and All Saints' Road.
ts' Road and Hale's Road.
Road and Cemetery. } **1d.**

n Brooklyn and Tennyson Roads and Colonnade.
wn Hotel and All Saints' Road.
llier Rotunda and Hale's Road.
de and Cemetery } **3d.**

n Brooklyn and Tennyson Roads and Hale's Road.
wn Hotel and Cemetery. } **5d.**

g Summer Months Saturday and Sunday Service extended until 8-30
from Tennyson Road, 9 o'clock from Cemetery.

FARES continued

Junction Brooklyn and Tennyson Roads and Lansdown Hotel
L.M.S. Station and Montpellier Rotunda.
Lansdown Hotel and Colonnade.
Montpellier Rotunda and All Saints' Road.
Colonnade and Hale's Road.
All Saints' Road and Cemetery } **2d.**

L.M.S. Station and All Saints' Road.
Lansdown Hotel and Hale's Road
Montpellier Rotunda and Cemetery.
Junction Brooklyn and Tennyson Roads and All Saints' Road. } **4d.**

Junction Brooklyn and Tennyson Roads and Cemetery. } **6d.**

Children Half-Fares.   Minimum 1d.
SUNDAY SERVICE as on Week-days from 2 o'clock.

The timetable for the St Mark's-Cemetery bus service of the 1920s.

Another gathering of the company's staff, taken in the late 1920s. Car no.22 is visible on the left, and one of the three rebuilds is on the right.

Two well turned out company employees c.1930. Driver Jim Fletcher and Conductor Frank Wood had taken a short break from crewing one of the early Guy single-deckers. Note Frank's bell-punch and whistle. Until the early 1930s conductors used whistles to give instructions to the drivers; bells eventually replaced them.

Nine
The End of Tramway Operations

Concerns over the condition of the tramway had begun to become widespread in the later 1920s; there had been virtually no investment in the system since the delivery of the three 1921 cars. The council had made its view regularly known to the company but were rather taken aback when late in 1928 they received a copy of a draft of the Cheltenham District Traction Bill which the company had drawn up. This would empower the company inter alia to run trolleybuses and motor buses, and to change their name to that of the Cheltenham District Traction Co. The Bill envisaged trolleybuses not only running over all former tram routes but with extensions in a loop around St Mark's estate, along the full length of Old Bath Road, from High Street along Tewkesbury Road and from Six Ways to East End in Charlton Kings.

From the outset the council decided to oppose the Bill in every possible way. Their concern related specifically to the operation of trolleybuses, and in particular to the spread of overhead wires through many streets of the town, particularly as such vehicles required two wires, instead of the single wires of the tramway system. The town's Chamber of Commerce had previously planned to support the Bill on the basis that trolleybuses would only appear on the former tram routes; they now gave their full backing to the council's line. In February the National Citizens' Union took out an advertisement in the *Gloucestershire Echo* to encourage 'all owners and rate-payers' to support the council in its opposition. By the end of that month it was noted that petitions in opposition to the Bill had been deposited with the House of Lords by Gloucestershire County Council, Charlton Kings Urban District Council, Cheltenham Town Council, Cheltenham Rural District Council, the GWR, the LMSR and the BTCC. So great was the council's disapproval that additional funds were approved in order that all appropriate legal action might be taken to oppose the Bill. In presenting its case for change, the company reported some interesting facts:

i) The annual number of passenger journeys had fallen from a peak of 3million to 2.3million and as a consequence receipts had fallen from about 18d per car mile to 14½d.
ii) Expenses were running at 13d per car mile – profits were therefore minimal and there had been no dividends for shareholders since 1925.
iii) Each tram was covering an average of 4,000 miles each year.
iv) Electricity payments to the council averaged £3,500 per annum.
v) Infrastructure maintenance was costing 2d per tram mile.

By April, the council had resolved to exercise its powers to purchase the tramway and to continue to oppose the Traction Bill. However all this was to change at a subsequent meeting with the company which produced an unexpectedly rapid and amicable agreement: the trams would be withdrawn and all town services would in future be operated by motor buses. The Mayor expressed his delight, along with the hope that the arrangement would be beneficial both to the town and the company. The Chamber of Commerce was quick to congratulate the council on the success of its opposition to the Bill, and to finding a workable alternative.

At the May meeting of the GPWC, the company confirmed its willingness to proceed quickly with the conversion of the system but sought prior reassurance that the council would not now be taking any steps to purchase the system when that option next fell due, on 31 December 1931. The Town Council met with the company to discuss this. It was agreed that the council would not further consider the purchase option for 1931 and also that the company would first introduce buses on the Leckhampton and Prestbury Road routes, and that this would happen within six months. As will be explained in Chapter 11, the buses were quickly ordered, but not without some further exchanges with the council. By September the company was suggesting that Leckhampton should not after all be first to enjoy the buses. It was agreed to wait until the next year before buses started on that route as the roads would need new asphalt once the tram lines had been taken up, and such work could not be done in winter.

At a meeting with the Streets and Highways Committee on 17 February 1930 it was reaffirmed that the agreement with the company was as follows:

i)   Operation of trams would cease on the Cleeve Hill and and Leckhampton routes not later than 31 March 1930, and on all other routes (ie Lansdown-Charlton Kings) by 31 March 1931.
ii)   The council and the company would agree precise dates nearer the time.
iii) Any tram poles required by the council for other purposes would be left in situ.
iv)   The council would not seek to purchase the system in 1931.

The cost of reinstatement of the highways was considerable; it was announced later that year that reinstatement of the Leckhampton route, for example, required attention to 10,519 sq.yds of roadway at a cost of £2,892 14s 6d. The following year it was agreed that the Acme Flooring & Paving Co. would begin work on reinstating the High Street with wood block paving for an agreed total of £10,401 5s.

With the gradual wind-down of the system and an even more gradual phasing in of motor buses as is described in Chapter 11, there was no celebration of the final day of tramway operation. The last trams ran, as planned, from Leckhampton and Cleeve Hill on 31 March 1930; the final car was brought down from Cleeve Hill by motorman Harry Walters, who had also been privileged to take the first service car up the hill almost twenty-nine years earlier. The last service car left Charlton Kings on 31 December that same year. The *Echo* for 5 January 1931 reported as follows:

Trams Pass Out of the Running in Cheltenham.

The Cheltenham trams have passed quietly away. There might be another kick or so in the old bones but to all intents and purposes the trams are dead. Only one set of tram lines is now in existence, from Charlton Kings to the LMS station – and these will be taken up shortly.

For some time the tram has been running twice a day on this route to preserve the company's right to use the track. After the last day of 1930 this service was stopped but it is possible that for a short time a tram will be used occasionally to keep the line down.

The removal of the lines in St George's Road and Clarence Street began in March 1931 and at the Streets and Highways Committee meeting the following July it was noted that all lines had been removed and all roads reinstated. The company was to be reminded to remove the final poles not required by the council for street lighting purposes.

Some 175 electric tramway systems has operated in Great Britain and Northern Ireland; closures had generally commenced in the late 1920s and around thirty systems had ceased operations before that in Cheltenham. By contrast, that in Blackpool is still in operation today, and several cities have in recent years re-introduced street tramways, although very different to the ones of the early twentieth century. Reference was made in Chapter 2 to the horse-drawn tramways in both Gloucester and Worcester; these were both converted to electrical operation in 1904 and remained iopen until 1933 and 1928 respectively.

Inspecting the withdrawn cars in 1931 are some prominent tramway enthusiasts. From left: F.M. Butterfield, L.B. Lapper, C.F. Klapper, D.J. Bastin, A.E. Broad and G.H. Hay. Of these Leslie Lapper was to become a co-founder of the Railway Correspondence and Travel Society and was a prominent photographer of the local transport scene; many of his bus photographs appear both in this book and its companion work, Cheltenham's Buses 1939-1980. C.F. Klapper was a founder member of the Omnibus Society and took several of the tramway photographs that appear in the volume. The cars are nos 13 (left), and 12, in its final form as single-decker.
(Omnibus Society (C.F. Klapper))

Following cessation of operations, cars were parked at the depot while their fate was determined; seen alongside the depot is car no.3 in its later guise as a single-decker. The car ahead of it is believed to be no.4. The other single-deck conversion, no.12, is just visible to its right. (Omnibus Society (C F Klapper))

Tracks being lifted and the roadway reinstated in Leckhampton Road, near the previous tram terminus. (Gloucestershire Echo)

Track lifting in the town centre. The last rail being lifted from Clarence Street in April 1931. (Gloucestershire Echo)

Ten

Disposal of the Cars and Surviving Artifacts

Many of the cars were well and truly worn out by 1930 – indeed, as noted earlier, some had already been scrapped. Some of the later additions and the rebuilds were however still in good condition and could have been expected to see further service elsewhere. Initially all of the cars were parked up at St Mark's, with the siding at the side of the depot taking as many as it could accommodate in order to free up covered accommodation for the new buses. Some of the older cars were quickly broken up at the depot with any reusable parts being salvaged and sold on. The three 1921 cars, 21-23, four of the rebuilds, nos 1, 9, 10 and 16, along with at least nos 13 and 25 were retained much longer with the intention of being sold intact.

After several years of standing idle it had become clear that these cars never would run again; they generally suffered the same fate as the others in the fleet except that the bodies of most of these survivors were sold for a variety of uses in the surrounding area. Three of these became quite well known local landmarks. An orchard alongside the old A40 trunk road at Staverton is where no.22 served as a hen house for many years, finally being incinerated by its owner in the mid-1960s. No.21 was bought for use as a store-shed on a market garden in Swindon Village where it remained until 1962. The body of no.13, rebuilt to the extent that it was barely recognisable, was converted by the company for use as a passenger shelter at the Cleeve Hill bus terminus; it remained in use until replaced in 1970.

Among the surviving monuments to the town's tramways are four standards still in use for street lighting purposes in Prestbury Road, between Pittville Circus Road and Whaddon Road, and the impressive building in Clarence Street built to house the electricity generating plant. The building had in fact been built in 1895 to supply all of the town's electricity needs, although the tramway company quickly became the biggest single customer.

More than a hundred yards of tram track are also still thought to exist covered by a thin layer of tarmac along the approach road to what is now the Stagecoach bus depot at St Mark's. The tracks were fully exposed until resurfacing of the lane took place in the early 1960s. While in theory the tram shed still exists, the extent of its expansion and modernisation has been such that very little of the original structure now remains. In 1940, for example, the west wall was removed and the depot extended to encompass the strip of land on which the open siding had previously stood; a few years later the whole of the roof structure was replaced. Alongside the depot is the small office originally used by the Manager; although it has over the years lost its bay window and 'front' door, it still proudly displays the letters 'CDLR' in its stonework.

At the Holy Apostles junction a chamber still exists beneath the pavement; this is understood to have housed equipment for boosting the power supply to cars using the Charlton Kings line.

But the most important survivor is car no.21 itself. As noted above it remained at Boote's Farm in Swindon Village until 1962. Its removal did not mark its end; in fact it gave it a new beginning. During 1961 the car was purchased by local tramway enthusiasts, who formed the Cheltenham 21 Tram Group. The car had been protected from the elements while on the farm by a corrugated metal roof; nevertheless, it needed much restoration. The initial work was carried out in situ but the car was transported to a yard in Leckhampton in 1962, where, over a three-year period, much more work was undertaken. In 1965, no.21, by then looking very respectable, was transported to the National Tramway Museum at Crich in Derbyshire, following a sentimental trip along the line of its former route to Charlton Kings. Ownership of the car was at that time transferred from the Cheltenham group to the Tramway Museum Society. Progress on the car at Crich was however minimal, largely because the museum's operational system is constructed to the standard gauge on which the Cheltenham car was unable to operate.

In May 1981, ownership of no.21 was transferred again, this time to Bournemouth Borough Council; no.21 was in due course removed to Bournemouth where it was stored under cover with the hope of a heritage tramway project coming to fruition in the South Coast resort. Eventually however it was recognised that neither accommodation for the project nor a suitable truck for no.21 would become available and in 1992 the car was offered to Cheltenham Borough Council who were pleased to accept the body of the car. Ownership was transferred accordingly and during May of that year the car returned to its home town where it is now in storage, awaiting a decision as to when a further round of restoration may begin. The car, which saw less than ten years of service, has now been in preservation for forty years; somewhat ironically it is now back in store just a few hundred yards from where it had spent thirty years on the market garden. We can only hope that one day the car will be fully restored to its former glory as a most fitting reminder of the town's electric tramway system.

The grand building erected in 1895 to house the Cheltenham Corporation's electricity generating plant; the building still stands proudly in Clarence Street, in the stretch known originally as Manchester Street, although its history will be largely unknown to the thousands who pass along this busy thoroughfare each day. The tramways were dependent upon this facility for their power. The importance of the building to the town's heritage has recently been recognised by the fitting on its east wall of a plaque. Upon this, the Cheltenham Civic Society and the Gloucestershire Society for Industrial Archaeology jointly record that 'this electricity sub-station was part of Cheltenham's first electricity supply in 1895. Its design was based on the Strozzi Palace in Florence. 2000 volts were transformed to 100 volts at the unusual frequency of 94 Hertz.'

Four tram standards still remain in use for lighting purposes in the stretch of Prestbury Road between Pittville Circus and Whaddon Road; they are now 100 years old. A modern Stagecoach bus (above) passes beneath them on its way to Lynworth, while, below, a newly erected Stagecoach bus stop provides an interesting contrast in design styles of street furniture over a hundred year period.

The body of car no.13 formed the basis of a bus shelter which until 1970 stood at the Cleeve Hill bus terminus. Probably very little of the original body remained when this view was taken near to the end of the shelter's life.

In this photograph taken in November 1986, the National Bus Co. logo on a Leyland National bus makes a curious contrast with the initials of the Cheltenham & District Light Railway which still remain today on the face of the original office at St Mark's depot.

Old cars just fade away. After failing to find a buyer for further service, the body of car no.22 was removed to an Orchard at Staverton where it stood as a well-known landmark alongside the old A40 for thirty years. It is seen above in the 1950s with only a few hens for company – its main role was to provide them with a home. By the early 1960s, the old car had all but disintegrated, as shown below. (John Appleby)

Car no.21 was to be the one that got away – from the scrap man that is. When eventually sold by the company c.1932, the body of the car was purchased by the Boote family and moved to their small holding at Huntscot Farm, located off Kingsditch Lane, on the corner of what is now Running's Road. The car was used primarily for storing crates used for the transport of the family's produce; considerable forethought by the new owners led to a pitched corrugated metal roof being erected above the car's top deck. It was to be this structure which was to ensure the car's long term future. The car was rescued for preservation in 1961. The car is seen above late in 1961, with the protective roof still in place, and initial restoration work under way. (21 Tram Group)

Well-known local hauliers, Elliott Bros, were engaged to move the car to Leckhampton on 14 April 1962. Here 1961 Bedford TK tractor unit 7431 AD eases the car out of Huntscot Farm, and onto the highway for the first time in thirty years. (21 Tram Group)

As it left its home of thirty years, no.21 posed briefly in Kingsditch Lane alongside one of the town's newest buses, 1961 Bristol FSF 6036 (801 MHW), diverted specially for a couple of minutes from its duties on Service 6 to Swindon Village, along with some understanding passengers! The town was to receive many buses of Bristol manufacture in the 1950s and 1960s; their history is recorded in the companion volume, Cheltenham's Buses 1939 – 1980.

Back in the town centre after thirty-five years: following three years of restoration in Leckhampton, no.21 was ready to be transported to the National Tramway Museum at Crich in Derbyshire. Before leaving the town the vehicle was exhibited briefly in the town centre, and then made a triumphant run over the former Charlton Kings tram route. Elliott Bros again provided transport, this time with 1965 TK tractor unit EDF353C. The Cheltenham District Traction Co. provided their newest Bristol FLF, 7185 (BHY716C), to accompany no.21 on the tour through town. Here the vehicles stand in Clarence Street, attracting much interest from passers-by on 10 July 1965. (21 Tram Group)

Following some years in store at Crich, no.21 moved to Bournemouth. Here two generations of preserved Cheltenham transport are seen at that town's Mallard Road bus garage during an enthusiasts' open day. 1967 Bristol RELL 1003 (KHW309E), then owned by the Cheltenham Bus Preservation Group, stands alongside no.21 in July 1984. (Dave Russell/Deric Pemberton)

No.21 returned to Cheltenham in 1992 and is now in secure storage. Its top deck fittings had to be removed for it to enter the building in which it currently resides. This photograph was taken in February 2001.

Eleven

Motor Buses Take Over

In the years before implementation of the 1930 Road Traffic Act, the licensing of buses, as with all other Hackney carriages, was in the gift of individual local authorities. While some councils chose not to exercise those powers, Cheltenham certainly did. They included the authorisation of local bus services, the places at which they could pick up or set down, the number of vehicles operated and their fitness for use. Thus, although the Town Council had been actively seeking the abandonment of the tramways and their replacement with buses, Cheltenham District was still required to apply formally to that same body for permission to operate buses within the town.

At the 2 August 1929 meeting of the town's General Purposes and Watch Committee, the Traction Co.'s request for licences for ten double-deck tram-replacement buses was considered. A somewhat shocked committee made it clear that in their view single-deckers should be quite adequate to meet the needs of the town. In reviewing the business of that committee at a full meeting of the Town Council on 2 September, it transpired that, keen as the councillors were to see the end of the trams, its members had in general shared the committee's assumption that the replacement vehicles would be of single-deck construction. Some councillors were clearly aghast at the prospect of double-deck vehicles running on the town's streets – claiming that they would be 'even more of an eyesore than the trams' as they went about their business in the town's Regency thoroughfares. Fortunately other council members were a little more objective. They came to the company's defence by pointing out that single-deckers would be unable to cope with the loadings on many routes, with the consequence either that passengers would be left standing at their stops, or that duplicate vehicles would have to be operated, bringing even more buses onto the town's streets. The discussion came to a somewhat abrupt close when Councillor Winterbotham, clearly better-informed on these matters than many of her colleagues, pointed out that the council in fact had no power of veto over this issue. Indeed, the buses had already been ordered to ensure their availability within the timescale agreed with the council!

While local folklore has it that, in view of their concerns, the council insisted that any double-deckers should be of the open-top variety, this in reality appears not to have been true; the council simply needed convincing that double-deckers of any sort were appropriate. As the company had already ordered the vehicles before this debate had taken place, it must be assumed that it was they who had opted for open-top bodywork. While it is possible that they had anticipated the council's concerns, their choice was more likely to have been influenced by the lower capital cost of such vehicles and, maybe to a point, the greater fuel economy which would have resulted from the reduction in overall weight.

On 4 September 1929, just two days after the council meeting, the Traction Co. announced that a deal had been struck with Guy Motors for the delivery of twenty vehicles, at an average cost of £2,000. Ten of these would be double-deckers, due for delivery at the end of that month. The balance of the order, to be taken over the next few years, was expected to be split equally between double-deck and single-deck vehicles (as things were to turn out, all but one of the later deliveries were single-deckers). Taking its lead from the Town Council, the company reassured the public that the vehicles would not be visually intrusive; they would be 'of a low-loading type, not more than 10ft 6in in height'. They were also quick to stress, as a major plus point, their ability to make the climb up Cleeve Hill at 20mph compared with the 8mph achieved by the trams.

Towards the end of November 1929 the eagerly-awaited motor buses arrived – two months later than expected. The ten vehicles in the initial batch were Invincible models with Guy's own bodywork. The Invincible had been launched in 1928 as Guy's standard 4-wheel forward-control double-deck chassis. Soon after the arrival of the vehicles in Cheltenham, no.10 was posed for photographs outside the offices of the *Gloucestershire Echo* and on 29 November that journal reported this significant event for the town in the following terms:

Our New Buses To Replace The Trams
Arrival of New Vehicles in Cheltenham

The first consignment of ten of the double-decker 'buses which are to supersede the tram service in Cheltenham arrived at the depot at St Mark's on Friday afternoon, having made the journey by road from Guy's motor works at Wolverhampton earlier in the day.

The new 'buses are handsome-looking vehicles, painted in the company's colours of red and yellow, with the borough arms depicted on the side panels, together with the name of the Cheltenham District Traction Company. They are designed to carry fifty-one passengers, and, being fitted with 56hp six cylinder engines, they run with beautiful smoothness; they are fitted with Dunlop pneumatic tyres, one in front and twin in rear.

The top deck is open to the sky. The buses will seat twenty-four downstairs and twenty-seven upstairs. The full weight of the buses loaded will be 9tons; unloaded and equipped ready for use they weigh 5tons and 14cwt. They are built very low to the road and there is a very wide platform for getting on and off. Each is beautifully upholstered in leather.

After a brief rest at the depot the fleet came out and made a tour of the proposed service routes to Charlton Kings, Cleeve Hill and other outlying districts, being much admired by the spectators en route. The 'buses took Cleeve Hill particularly well.

The fleet numbers allocated to these Invincibles logically followed on from those of the existing Guy single-deckers and thus they entered service as nos 6-15. They were registered DF 8900-8909. Initially route information showed no improvements over that of the trams, with a small box in the front canopy large enough only to show the ultimate destination. Very early on in their lives route number boxes were added, to be followed by 'via' boards which were hung from the front rails on the top deck to display the principal intermediate stops. By December 1929 the vehicles had become a familiar site on the Cleeve Hill, Lansdown Castle and Leckhampton routes which they shared with the remaining trams until replacing them completely in March of the following year. This gradual introduction fortuitously allowed for the retraining of tram drivers in order that they could take control of the new fleet. During October, the Cheltenham Corporation had approved the issue of licences to thirty-three of the company's drivers and conductors.

The vehicles were essentially dark red, but with their windows and canopy picked out in cream (or yellow as the press report has it). The upper deck side panels were initially also of a light colour (maybe cream, although photographic evidence suggests a different shade or colour) but within a year or so, these panels were repainted red and advertisements were applied. The lower red panels were neatly lined out.

While there were still many open-top double-deck buses in use around the country at that time, they were by then generally the older vehicles in most fleets; closed-top vehicles had appeared in large numbers from the mid-1920s and were now accepted as the norm. Indeed, just eighteen months after these Guys had entered service in the town, the Western National Omnibus Co. began to use closed-top double-deckers on some of the workings on its service from Stroud into Cheltenham. Their introduction appears not to have ruffled the council's feathers, although in fairness these vehicles may not have appeared in the town on a regular basis. It is perhaps relevant to record that the very last new open-top double-deck vehicles delivered anywhere in the UK for normal service use (as opposed to sea-front and other tourist purposes) were supplied in 1932 – surprisingly for service in London, where closed-top vehicles had already been operating for a number of years.

Cheltenham District's customers were however no doubt delighted that the trams were finally being replaced with something rather more modern, and at first would have shared the excitement clearly apparent in the *Echo* report. After the initial euphoria had passed and the reality of the British weather had been considered, how pleased the passengers really were with the continued use of open-top transport is something seemingly not recorded, at least not until 1934. Although the press report generously described them as 'handsome-looking', Cheltenham's new buses did in fact look somewhat antiquated, even by the standards of 1929 – and not just by reason of their open-tops; their overall design in some respects appeared rather more primitive than that of the tramcars.

Another open-top Invincible arrived in April 1930; this vehicle however had already seen service elsewhere. PG 5606 had been a Guy Motors' demonstrator which had been registered in Surrey at the start of a period of loan to East Surrey Motors. It had first taken to the road in 1929, having left the Guy works just ahead of Cheltenham's Invincible order; on arrival in the town it became no.16. Its fifty-four-seat body by Hall Lewis was to a more modern-looking design, incorporating for example an enclosed rear staircase. Its livery was red, but with three distinct cream bands, one each above and below the lower deck windows, with the third around the top of the upper deck side panels. Its destination equipment was more passenger-friendly than that on the Guy bodies as a route number box was provided atop a main box listing two intermediate stopping places in addition to the ultimate destination.

The Invincible chassis proved to be well-engineered and robust; in fact these Guys were in some ways perhaps to prove too durable as, with rapid advances in vehicle design, they were almost obsolete before taking to the road. Withdrawals began in December 1935, and the last to run in its original form came off the road in August 1938. While one or two were possibly used as a source of spares, six were given new bodies by Beadle, all to much improved designs. Details of these new bodies, along with those of the complex renumbering which most of these vehicles underwent, appear later in this chapter.

As the final trams were about to disappear from the Charlton Kings route at the end of 1930, a fleet of eight Guy Conquests arrived; the Conquest was the normal control version of the Invincible, intended for the fitting of single-deck bodies. The Cheltenham vehicles did indeed carry such bodies, once again built by Guy, and to a much more attractive design than the Invincibles of only eleven months earlier; the Conquests arrived in town in October 1930. The vehicles were numbered 17-24 and registered DG 1310-1317. These twenty-eight-seat forward-entrance saloons were finished in red below their windows and cream above. Like the original Invincibles, the destinations were again of the single-line pattern, and again route number boxes were fitted soon after their arrival in the town. The route number was also displayed in the central rear windows of these Conquests. The first three windows on each side of their bodies were opening half-drops.

In a statement to the *Gloucestershire Echo* on 22 November, the company expressed the hope that this new fleet would be on the road by 1 December. It was reported that they would enable a more frequent and a quicker service on all routes, as well as proving more comfortable for passengers in the winter months – the first acknowledgement that open-toppers were after all not ideal. The General Manager stressed that, in selecting these single-deckers, passengers' comfort 'had been studied to the fullest degree; a central gangway of ample width is flanked by artistically placed seats. The roof is high enough to allow a six-foot man to stand in comfort'. Smoking was to be permitted only in the back seats. The vehicles were powered by the same Guy six-cyclinder engines as in the Invincibles, thereby ensuring a favourable power:weight ratio. A high price was inevitably to be paid for this in terms of fuel economy; it is understood that less than six miles per gallon was achieved!

Attractive as these vehicles might have been, their stay in Cheltenham was generally short-lived, quite probably because they were too small to cope with the loadings on many of the workings and therefore impeded overall flexibility in vehicle deployment. In 1934 new homes were readily found within the Balfour Beatty group for five of these Conquests, with nearby Stratford Blue and the neighbouring Leamington & Warwick Co. The three which remained in Cheltenham (nos 20-22) were withdrawn and sold for scrap in December 1938.

The twentieth of the Guys to arrive under the original agreement with the manufacturer was a very unusual vehicle – but nevertheless a popular one with summer day-trippers up to Cleeve Hill. This vehicle was not an open-topper but an open-sider, better known as a toast-rack. It arrived in the town in May 1932, numbered 25 and registered DG 4474. The vehicle had an Invincible forward-control chassis. The thirty-five-seat toast-rack body was again built by Guy Motors. It was fitted with canvas sheets along its sides which could be drawn in the event of a sudden down-pour and a horizontal rail ran the length of the off-side to prevent passengers falling into the road. So unusual was this vehicle that more photographs appear to have been taken of it than any other vehicle in the fleet. Most of these capture it with the additional decoration that it carried for the silver jubilee of King George V and Queen Mary in 1935.

While the vehicle might have been fun for passengers, it was quite a challenge for its conductors. There was no central gang-way as each row of seats was individually accessed from the full length step along the nearside of the vehicle; the only way of moving from row-to-row was to scramble along this step while hanging on to the rails and seats. Len Edwards, who started service as a conductor before progressing through the ranks of Driver, Inspector and Senior Inspector to eventually become the Cheltenham Depot Traffic Superintendent, remembers falling off this vehicle while it was ascending Cleeve Hill and having to pursue it to its next stop before resuming his duties. Although the vehicle cannot have covered a huge mileage as its usage was governed by the weather, it was a victim of the outbreak of war, non-essential vehicles not having a place in such conditions. The toast-rack thus departed the town late in 1939.

The four original Guy saloons dating from 1924/25 had reached the end of their useful lives by 1932 and were withdrawn. The fleet numbers of two of these, nos 1 and 2, were now re-allocated to a pair of second-hand Guy ONDs acquired as replacements. They had been new in 1928 to a small Warwickshire company, Reliance of Bidford-on-Avon, but had become surplus to requirements when that company was purchased by Stratford Blue; the Stratford company therefore sought a new home for the pair within the Balfour Beatty group. Thus UE 9319 and 9816 came to Cheltenham in June 1932, becoming nos 2 and 1 respectively. They were smaller vehicles than any others within the town, seating only twenty in their forward-entrance Guy-built bodies. They were however big enough to cope with the normal loadings on services to Sandy Lane and the weekly market in Gloucester Road. They remained in the town for about five years. Destination information was displayed in the same manner as the Guy Conquests. In 1934 they were re-numbered 19 and 18 respectively to make way for the next generation of double-deckers.

Thus for the summer of 1932 the fleet comprised the following twenty-three vehicles:

1, 2	UE 9816, 9319	Guy OND/Guy single-deck
5	RA 4210	Guy B/Guy single-deck
6-15	DF 8900 – 8909	Guy Invincible/Guy open-top double-deck
16	PG 5606	Guy Invincible/Hall Lewis open-top double-deck
17-24	DG 1310 – 1317	Guy Conquest/Guy single-deck
25	DG 4474	Guy Invincible/Guy single-deck toast-rack

Having thus reviewed the developments in the motor bus fleet over the first two full years since tramway abandonment, this is a convenient juncture at which to review the developments that had occurred in the service network over that same period. While initially the bus routes had represented a more-or-less straight replacement of the tram services, along with a continuation of the earlier two bus services, the services were subjected to considerable experimentation for several years before a settled pattern began to emerge. The November 1931 timetable listed the following services:

1   St Mark's (Brooklyn Road)-Lansdown Castle-LMS Station-Calcutta-GWR Station-Centre-Pittville Gates-Oaklands-Prestbury-Southam-Cleeve Hill.
1A   As above but via the Gas Works instead of GWR Station.
2   Lilleybrook-Charlton Kings (Cirencester Road/Bradley Road)-Lyefield Road-Six Ways-Centre-GWR Station-Calcutta-LMS Station-Lansdown Castle-St Mark's (Shops).
3   Maud's Elm-Marsh Villa-St Pauls Road-Centre-Bath Road-Norwood Arms -Leckhampton Road-Pilley Bridge-Leckhampton (Foot of Hill).
4   LMS Station-Tivoli-Park Place-Montpellier-Centre-Hewlett Road-Harp Hill-Cemetery.
5   Racecourse-Evesham Road-Centre-Montpellier-College-Thirlestaine Road-Sandy Lane.
6   St Mark's (Brooklyn Road/Tennyson Road)-Lansdown Castle-LMS Station-Calcutta-Gas Works-Centre-London Road-Old Bath Road-Pilley Bridge-Leckhampton (Foot of Hill).
7   Centre-GWR Station-Calcutta-LMS Station-Lansdown Castle-Shelburne Road-Hatherley Road-Hatherley (Coney Cree).

These routes required eighteen vehicles for normal afternoon operation. It should be noted that for some years morning services operated rather less frequently than those in the afternoons, additional vehicles coming onto the road from midday. That to Hatherley had been approved by the council in December 1930, while Service 3 between Maud's Elm and Leckhampton had received their blessing in February 1931. Subsequent applications were referred directly to the newly-appointed Traffic Commissioners in line with the requirements set out in the 1930 Road Traffic Act, although the Town Council was still advised of such applications in order that they might determine whether it would be appropriate to offer support, or to raise objections.

Some more important changes were made when, just three months later, the February 1932 timetable became effective. Route 1 continued to run to Cleeve Hill, but only from the Centre, while short workings to Prestbury (Shaw Green Lane) were now known as the 1A. Service 5 had been turned into an imaginative three-cornered route, for having travelled as before from Sandy Lane to the Racecourse it then returned to the LMS Station via the Centre and the Gas Works, returning to the Centre by the same route before heading back to Sandy Lane. Journeys to Hatherley now began at Leckhampton, but were subsumed into Service 6; thus all vehicles on that route travelled as far as Lansdown Castle, with some then heading for Hatherley and others to St Mark's.

For the July 1932 timetable, another community was to receive a service, this time by the diversion of some Service 2 journeys within Charlton Kings to East End instead of Lilleybrook; these were known as 2A. These changes had reduced the over-bussing of the St Mark's area apparent in the 1931 timetable and given a rather more even coverage across the town. A proposal by the company for an evening circular service around the town was not approved, but no objection was raised to the introduction of a service from the LMS Station to Whaddon Road football ground when Cheltenham Town Football Club was playing at home.

Some of the termini were on busy thoroughfares and required the vehicles to make some reversing manoeuvres which would be unthinkable in the traffic conditions of later years. Some of the Service 4 journeys, for example, terminated at the Gloucester Road entrance to Lansdown Station; the vehicles were required to reverse from that main thoroughfare into Libertus Road. Worse still, the Lilleybrook terminus was at the eastern entrance to the Lilleybrook Hotel; the buses were required to pull onto the wrong side of the main Cirencester Road before reversing into the Hotel entrance. On one occasion one of the 1940 Albion Venturers had its side ripped out by a passing lorry while turning at this point.

The East End and Hatherley services cannot have been successful as they were quickly phased out. As both destinations were already served by Bristol Tramways country services as they headed out of town en route to Oxford and Gloucester respectively, it seems likely that there was insufficient demand to justify retention of the town services along the same routes. Both suburbs were eventually to reappear on the CDT route map, although not until the late 1940s. However in 1933, a Thursdays-only service, reusing number 7, was introduced between the town centre and the Calcutta via the Gas Works, in order to serve the weekly market held in Gloucester Road.

Much of the credit for the relatively smooth transition from trams to buses must lie with Henry McCormick who had been with the undertaking since the inauguration of the tram services. His job cannot at times have been easy as he attempted to meet the demands of the council while at the same time both operating within the constraints that that same body imposed and achieving an appropriate level of profit for his masters. McCormick retired as General Manager in 1932 but stayed on in the town until his death in 1944. He was succeeded by Eric Sleight who had been manager of Carlisle's tramways until their closure towards the end of 1931. The Carlisle undertaking had also been part of the Balfour Beatty group.

Before his retirement McCormick addressed a meeting of the National Citizens' Union. He assured them that plans were in hand to improve the destination information displayed by vehicles, with boards being prepared for both the front and rear of the vehicles. Presumably these were the 'via' boards already mentioned as being hung from the top deck rails of the 1929 Invincibles. He went on to assure his audience that bells would shortly be replacing the whistles used by conductors.

Following an approach by disgruntled passengers, fed up with having to sit on crowded lower decks during periods of inclement weather, the Town Council decided to support their plea for better vehicles. At their meeting in February that year, the General Purposes and Watch Committee asked Cheltenham District to acquire closed top double-deckers for use on Charlton Kings and Leckhampton services at the earliest opportunity. The Traction Co. expressed a willingness to acquire such vehicles in the longer term, but pointed out that as its existing fleet was still relatively new, such progress would not be rapid. The company did however quickly place an order for six AEC Regent petrol-engined vehicles to be delivered with Weymann fifty-four-seat bodies. These very attractive vehicles took to the road in September 1934. Fleet numbers again reverted to 1, the batch thus being numbered 1-6, with registrations DG 9818-9823. They were therefore some of the very last vehicles registered by the Gloucestershire County Council motor taxation office with two-letter marks, AAD registrations commencing just a few days later. To make way for these in the numerical sequence, the ex-Reliance Guy saloons 1 and 2 (UE 9816, 9319) were re-numbered 18 and 19, as mentioned above, and open-top DF 8900 (formerly no 6) became number 17. These numbers had in turn been among those freed up by the departure of five of the Guy Conquests earlier in the year. No. 5 (RA 4210), the ex-Hayton Guy saloon, had also completed its service in the town just before the Regents arrived. Thus these new double-deckers had effectively replaced six Guy single-deckers, leaving the open-top double-deck fleet intact – not quite what the council had intended!

98

AEC had introduced the Regent in 1929 and it was to become one of the classics of its time. Balfour Beatty had ordered thirty-four Regents in 1932, largely to replace trams in Mansfield, and were clearly pleased with these. The Cheltenham vehicles wore the traditional colours; cream surrounded the lower deck windows in generous bands and also appeared as a band below the upper deck windows; the roofs were finished in silver. The vehicles were generously lined-out. Destinations were displayed in a large box showing ultimate and intermediate points, alongside a route number box. A large one-piece box appeared over the platform and a route number box was fitted at the rear.

The AEC Gazette, produced by the manufacturer for publicity purposes, reported that with the arrival of the Regents 'resplendent in red and cream livery, comfortable to a degree, and smooth and silent in operation, the council gave their warm-hearted approval to covered top double-deck saloon buses, an action which a discriminating public speedily endorsed'.

As part of his researches for the preparation of the article the AEC journalist also learned that at that time (1934) the total Cheltenham District route mileage stood at 22, with service 2 at 5.2 miles being the longest. The company's workforce then numbered seventy men and eleven boys, seven of who were employed as messengers for the thriving parcels service.

This is perhaps an appropriate juncture at which to comment further on the parcels service. As noted in Chapter 6, the service had originated in the early tramway days. It had proved successful from the outset and a van and a fleet of delivery bicycles were in constant use by the messengers mentioned above. Parcels were delivered within the town on behalf of a number of businesses, Cavendish House, the town's largest store, being a major customer. In the mid-1930s a major boost to the parcels service occurred when an agreement was made with the Red Arrow Parcels Co. for the Traction Co. to become one of its agents. This allowed the nightly transfer of parcels to and from the Red Arrow trunk service passing through the town. Parcels could therefore be despatched to any location in the country. The service continued to operate from the company's office in North Street, but, despite its continued success, ceased when its resources were needed for more pressing purposes during the war years; it was never re-instated.

So successful and popular were the 1934 Regents that six more vehicles to a similar specification arrived in January/February 1936. In fact, the appearance of this batch was a little different, as a consequence of the fitting of more informative destination indicators; in these later vehicles the ultimate destination was shown in a separate box from that listing the intermediate stopping points. They also seated fifty-six, two more than the 1934 vehicles. This delivery represented a serious attempt to replace the first of the 1929 Invincibles. Although it was to cause more than a little disruption to the numbering of the fleet, it was decided that these new vehicles would most logically be identified as 7-12; they received registrations BAD 27-32. The original no.9 (open-top DF 8903) had been taken out of service at the end of 1935, possibly as a source of spares for the others. Four of its siblings, nos 7, 8, 10 and 12 (DF 8901/2/4/6) appear to have been rendered surplus by these new arrivals and to have gone into limbo while their futures were decided. Number 11 (DF 8905) continued in use for a few more months, but was renumbered 18 to make way for the Regents. This number had been freed up by the withdrawal of one of the pair of UE-registered Guy ONDs, UE 9816.

Six of the Invincibles were in due course sent to Beadles at Dartford in Kent for new bodies to be fitted; three of those rebuilt became single-deckers. The new bodies on DF 8901/2/4 seated thirty-one, and they incorporated rear entrances, fitted with sliding doors. In their new form they were finished in red below the waist, and cream above; a cream flare also swept down from the waist to the rear wheel arches. Destination indicators were to a much improved layout, the route number being displayed alongside a box sufficiently large to accommodate the ultimate destination and two intermediate calling points. Three half-drop windows were included on each side of the saloon body. It appears that the return of these vehicles provided some additional capacity in the fleet, there having been no departures at that time. These three rebuilds did however need new fleet numbers as their previous identities had been taken by the Regents; thus DF 8901/2/4 became 18, 23 and 24 respectively. No.24 was transferred out of the fleet in 1940, but the other two are thought to have stayed for several more years, maybe as late as 1944.

Incredibly for that time, the other three rebuilds, DF 8905/6/9, were again to appear as open-top double-deckers. Why open-toppers should have been specified as late as 1937 is something of a mystery. It may have been that their use on the Cleeve Hill service was seen as something of a justification for this low-cost attempt at rejuvenation – indeed the trio split their time between the Cleeve Hill service, and that between Maud's Elm and the Cemetery. The bodies seated fifty-six and were of an altogether much improved design, incorporating enclosed staircases. Like the single-deck rebuilds, three half-drop windows were fitted each side and improved destination displays were provided. Livery was red with cream applied in a broad central band encompassing the lower deck windows surrounds. None of the rebuilds carried any lining-out, this attractive but expensive treatment having generally been dropped by this time. It is not entirely clear when these second-generation open-toppers finally left the fleet; it is however known that they had finally been withdrawn by the end of 1941. The re-entry into service of the three 'new' open-toppers brought about the withdrawal of two more of the remaining original open-toppers, 13 and 14 (DF 8907/8). As with the single-deck rebuilds, two of these returning open-toppers also needed new fleet numbers; thus DF 8905/6 now appeared as 13 and 14.

It is apparent from the two previous paragraphs that DF 8905 carried three different fleet-numbers in a little over a year (11, 18 and most recently 13). Conversely, fleet no.18 had been carried by three different vehicles in just a few months: Guy OND UE 9816, original open-topper DF 8905 and single-deck rebuild DF 8901. While there may have been some merit in keeping fleet numbers within a tight numerical range, such frequent re-numbering cannot have made vehicle identification particularly easy for maintenance or operating staff. Not surprisingly therefore, this practice was dropped in 1938, with all subsequent vehicles following a much simpler one-up number sequence.

The fleet total of twenty-five operational vehicles represented an increase of two compared with 1932; at the end of 1937 the stock list was as follows:

1-6	DG 9818 - 9823	AEC Regent/Weymann double-deckers
7-12	BAD 27 - 32	AEC Regent/Weymann double-deckers
13-14	DF 8905/6	Guy Invincible/Beadle open-top rebuild
15	DF 8909	Guy Invincible/Beadle open-top rebuild
16	PG 5606	Guy Invincible/Hall Lewis open-top
17	DF 8900	Guy Invincible/Guy open-top
18	DF 8901	Guy Invincible/Beadle single-deck rebuild
19	UE 9319	Guy OND/Guy single-decker
20-22	DG 1313 - 1315	Guy Conquest/Guy single-decker
23-24	DF 8902/4	Guy Invincible/Beadle single-deck rebuild
25	DG 4474	Guy Invincible/Guy toast-rack

A new purchase in April 1938 was a Bedford WTB, which took fleet no.19 from the vehicle it replaced, Guy OND UE 9319. Bedford had introduced the WT range of goods and passenger chassis in 1933; these took the manufacturer's goods models into the three-ton range for the first time and allowed those chassis fitted with passenger bodies to accommodate up to twenty-six seats. The Cheltenham example however seated only twenty in a Duple Hendonian coach body. This 26hp WTB, registered CDG 246, had been acquired primarily to operate a service introduced in 1937 between the town centre and the junction of Arle Road and Brooklyn Road. The service, numbered 8, turned out to be a great success. Although initially only operated on Saturdays it was soon upgraded to run six days each week, and the following year larger vehicles had to be substituted in order to cope with Saturday shoppers.

The vehicle was fitted with a route number box alongside an ultimate destination indicator; on its nearside it carried a slip board listing intermediate stopping places. The WTB was out-shopped in red with a cream bonnet top and waistband, the latter extending as a flare to skirt level behind the rear wheels. The Bedford was operated as a one-man vehicle but was to be a victim of the changed situation confronting the country in 1939 and left the Cheltenham fleet as that year drew to a close.

Two other departures at unknown dates, but believed to be towards the end of 1938, were the last two open-top Invincibles not to be rebuilt, 16 and 17 (PG 5606 and DF 8900). Also finishing their service at the same time were the final trio of Guy Conquest single-deckers, nos 20-22 (DG 1313-5). Their replacements were three AEC Regal 4s, transferred from Mansfield District, to whom they had been supplied new in June 1933. Registered AAL 108-110 they took numbers 27, 26 and 28 in the Cheltenham fleet, arriving in the town between November 1938 and February 1939. The Regal 4 was a relatively unusual model in the AEC range: less than 100 were produced. The '4' in its designation indicated that it was fitted with a four-cylinder engine. Like the AEC double-deckers, these transferred thirty-two-seat single-deckers had Weymann bodies, in this case with forward entrances and doors mounted at the top of their access steps. Sliding roofs had been specified by their original purchaser. Livery was red below the waist and cream above. Ultimate destinations were displayed alongside a route number box; and a route number was also displayed at the rear. Changing circumstances saw the Regals moving on again, leaving Cheltenham in 1940.

The Regals were not the only Mansfield vehicles to arrive at the end of 1938; with them came four more Regent double-deckers registered VO8585-8588. These were essentially identical to Cheltenham's own 1934 deliveries, but with the route number box mounted above a single-line front destination box. Destination boxes were also fitted over the platforms. They entered service in Cheltenham between November 1938 and February 1939, taking numbers 20, 21, 16 and 17 respectively, these numbers having been freed up by the recent withdrawals noted in the previous paragraph. These Regents were repainted to match the similar vehicles already in the fleet and in the process became the last Cheltenham vehicles to receive lining-out. These arrivals represented a net increase of two in fleet strength, in part attributable to the introduction of Service 9 – see below. A noteworthy feature of all sixteen of these Weymann-bodied Regents was that the drivers' cab doors were only partly glazed. This appears strange for these otherwise very up-to-date vehicles, and provides a reminder that, even in the mid-1930s, consideration of drivers' comfort did not feature highly in vehicle design.

The Regent fleet enjoyed a long life in Cheltenham. Although two of its members (nos 11 and 17) moved on to associated companies in 1944 and 1939 respectively, the remainder continued until routinely withdrawn between 1947 and 1951. The vehicles received no significant structural or mechanical modifications other than the fitting of diesel engines in place of the petrol units in the post-war years, by which time they had also received the post-war standard livery with much reduced cream, and red roofs. More details of these changes appear in the companion volume.

Following the experimentation of the early 1930s, the network of services had begun to settle down towards the middle of that decade. As noted above a new service numbered 8 first appeared in 1937 running from the town centre to the Arle Road/Brooklyn Road junction. In 1938 Service 9 was launched travelling from the Centre, along Whaddon Road to Cleeve View Road; within a year it had been extended to terminate at the Cemetery.

Thus the company had made steady progress in developing its route network and in updating its fleet of vehicles. But in 1939 Cheltenham District was to change hands; the company was to become a part of the Red and White United Transport group from 1 July of that year. *Cheltenham's Buses 1939 – 1980* follows the history of the town's bus operations through both the Red and White and the later Bristol Omnibus eras.

The initial tram replacement vehicles were ten Guy Invincibles, numbered 6-15 (DF 8900-8909); they are seen here late in 1929 before entering service, and almost certainly at the Guy works in Wolverhampton before delivery. (Author's collection)

Guy Invincible no.9 (DF 8903) speeds past sister no.11 (DF 8905) in Clarence Street; both vehicles are showing 'Race Course' on their destination blinds, but only one person appears to be on board. The sun is shining and the decorations are out for the 1935 Silver Jubilee, but the streets are strangely deserted.

No.7 (DF 8901) was photographed in the Colonnade c.1932. Note the box which was added over the front canopy early on in the vehicles' lives to display the service number, and the via board hanging from the top rail, in this case displaying 'Lansdown Castle'. The small destination box itself manages only to show 'L.M.S. & St Mark's'.

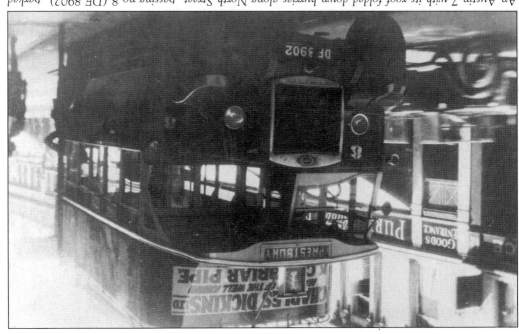

An Austin 7 with its roof folded down hurries along North Street, passing no.8 (DF 8902), parked outside the company's office and awaiting passengers for Prestbury on Service 1. The goods entrance to Boot's the Chemist is visible across the street. Although much modernised and extended, Boots is still on the same site today.

As noted in the text, once the ten Invincibles had arrived in the town in November 1929, they were presented to the local press. Number 10 (DF 8904) is seen in these two views outside the offices of The Gloucestershire Echo. The Echo was to remain in these offices until the 1990s, when it moved around the corner into Clarence Parade. The destination, set to read 'Special Bus', was particularly appropriate on this occasion. Note the Guy Motors' posters in the vehicle's windows – both the chassis and bodies had been built by the Wolverhampton company. The Indian chief's head, with full head-dress, used as an emblem by Guy for many years, may be seen atop the radiator, accompanied by the inscription 'Feathers in Our Cap'. Visible on the guard-rails are the Front Axle and Rear Axle Weights, together with the overall Unladen Weight, quoted as 5tons 8 Cwt 2 qrs. (Gloucestershire Echo)

The maximum permissible speed of 20mph is marked on the nearside guard rail of no. 10. With the vehicle in these two views are driver Arthur Higgs and Inspectors Bill Flook and Harvey Hales. The vehicle's road fund licence holder is mounted on the brackets supporting the front canopy. Note in the background the artistic ironwork on the Regency balconies of houses in Crescent Terrace, so typical of Cheltenham dwellings of that period. (Gloucestershire Echo)

Prestbury Road has occasionally flooded after heavy downpours, the rainwater readily finding its way down from Cleeve Hill. It was the water rather than the bus which attracted the photographer but the rear end features of the 1929 Invincibles may be clearly seen in this view of an amphibious no.8 (DF 8902), believed to have been taken in 1931. At that time the vehicle's upper panels were still finished in their original (cream?) colour. (Gloucestershire Echo)

A small group of passengers was waiting to board Invincible no.12 (DF 8906) in Park Place as it headed for the centre on Service 5 from Sandy Lane. Note the 'Local Buses Stop Here. Fare Stage' sign. Flags to this pattern remained in use until the late 1950s.

The Norwood Arms public house at the junction of Leckhampton and Shurdington Roads has been a well-known landmark for a very long time. It is on the right in this view, with its walls advertising the products of Flowers and Sons. The direction board indicates that Leckhampton Road takes motorists on to Stroud via Birdlip, whereas Shurdington Road would have taken them rather more directly to the same town albeit via Painswick. The railings on which the board is mounted prevent wayward passers-by from falling down the stairway leading to the gentlemen's toilets located below ground. The bus is Invincible no.11 (DF 8905) and it is heading for North Street in the town centre, having started its journey from the foot of Leckhampton hill. The via board shows that is has come via Charlton Lane. Two cyclists are also heading for the town centre on this sunny afternoon in the mid-1930s. Note the trough for drinking water for horses alongside the bus; these were familiar sites on main roads around the town until the 1960s. This particular example had been presented by the Cheltenham Ladies Society for the Protection of Animals late in the previous century and remains in situ today, now in use as a flower bed. Leckhampton Road had previously enjoyed tram services.

Ty-Phoo Tea and Timothy Whites were among the more regular advertisers during the 1930s. The 1929 Invincibles had had their upper panels painted red within two years of arriving in the town, and adverts were then quickly applied; this gave them a rather more solid appearance. No.14 (DF 8908) is seen in the Colonnade loading for a Service 4 journey to St Mark's via the LMS Station and Lansdown Castle. One of the small window vents is open in the lower saloon on what was clearly another sunny day; it is likely that a number of these vents were designed to open although with the open rear platforms fresh air would never have been in short supply. The sunny weather has also prompted the shop keepers to lower their sun blinds, and some passengers to brave the open deck. (Mike Rooum/PM Photography)

A very immodest advertisement for George's Grill Room seeks to tempt the public to their High Street premises. The shot of no.15 (DF 8909) is similar to that of no.14 above. The destination in this case unusually reads 'Tennyson Road' rather than St Mark's, although the two are generally synonymous. Note that the first digit in the fleet number is represented by a letter I rather than a figure 1; presumably there had been a shortage of transfers.

Number 16 (PG 5606) was the vehicle which arrived after short-term use as a Guy Motors' demonstrator, in which capacity it operated for East Surrey Motors. Its Hall Lewis body had a much more modern look than the other Invincibles, although all were built within weeks of each other. The bus is on a short-working of Service 4, set to terminate at Lyefield Road in Charlton Kings. The vehicle stands in the short stretch of the High Street between North Street (Boot's Corner) and Pittville Street. The Gloucestershire Dairy was advertising its safe milk – the company had one of the very first pasteurisation plants outside of London. The photograph is thought to date from the autumn of 1934.

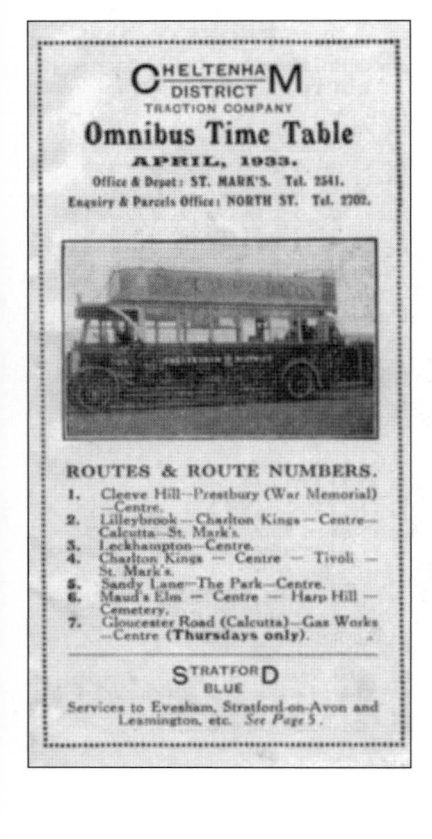

The 1929 Invincibles featured on the cover of the company's timetable booklets of the early 1930s; note too the reference to Stratford Blue, which during that period was also a member of the Balfour Beatty Group. From the mid-1930s, the company moved to timetable booklets with card covers, carrying an impression of a vehicle more similar to the 1937 rebuilds. Note the Borough arms, also of course carried on the vehicles, despite the company always having been in private ownership.

Three 1929 Invincibles were rebodied by John Beadle in 1937, with much more modern-looking double-deck bodies, but still with open tops. Here DF 8906, by this time re-numbered 14, negotiates the town centre roundabout, before pulling up at the North Street stop to load for another trip to Cleeve Hill on Service 1. The year is 1937; one of the AEC Regents delivered the previous year, no.9 (BAD 29), may be seen in the background loading for a Service 3 working to Leckhampton. The same Invincible is seen below at the Cleeve Hill terminus. The rear profile looked even more modern than its frontal appearance and incorporated a route number box.

Beadle also provided new bodies for three other 1929 Invincibles, but in these cases they reappeared as single-deckers. The retention of the short, high-mounted radiators did not help in any efforts to modernise the frontal profiles. The vehicles had three half-drop windows in each side, and sliding doors at their rear entrances. In these two views, no.23 (DF8902) is seen at the Cemetery terminus of Service 6, waiting to return to Maud's Elm. Its driver was Albert Slatter.

When two Guy ONDs arrived from the Reliance Bus Co. of Bidford-on-Avon in June 1932 they were numbered 1 and 2. Number 1 (UE 9816) is seen here in the Colonnade soon after arrival awaiting passengers for Sandy Lane on Service 5, one of its usual haunts. Note the side advertising boards. (Omnibus Society)

The other ex-Reliance OND was UE 9319, originally numbered 2, but re-numbered 19 in 1934. The vehicle awaits departure time for the Sandy Lane service outside Thomas Plant's in the Colonnade, with Invincible no.14 on Service 4 behind. Both vehicles have the drivers' windscreens open. The ONDs appear to have no other ventilation to offer their passengers; presumably the door was left ajar when things got uncomfortably warm. (Mike Rooum/PM Photography)

A delightful period scene in the mid-1930s. Three ladies demonstrate the fashions of the day as they queue to board Guy Conquest no 21 (DG 1314) as it heads for Maud's Elm on Service 6.

Soon after the Conquests arrived in Cheltenham, route number boxes were fitted atop their destination screens, and advertising boards were fitted above the side windows. No.20 (DG 1313) stands at the Service 6 stop outside Burton's, the outfitters. The premises of True Form and Maynards (on the corner of Regent Street) are also visible – all three names were to be found in many High Streets across the land. The Conquest will shortly be departing for Maud's Elm; it is being overtaken by a very solid-looking 1936 saloon car. (Mike Rooum/PM Photography)

Toast-track no.25 (DG 4474) seen on the High Street roundabout turning into The Colonnade. Both the vehicle and the town centre are decorated for the 1937 Coronation. The roundabout was built c.1935, a small fountain is operating in its centre, maybe as a temporary measure until the larger fountain could be installed. The rear end of an AEC Regent is visible in the background.

A little advertising licence was used when this photograph appeared in a national magazine in 1937 with the caption "A 1936 winter incident on a cross-country 'bus route'". The route was in fact Cheltenham District's Service 1 to Cleeve Hill, taken near the Rising Sun Hotel. Guy Conquest no.23 (DG 1316) is in trouble, possibly with a rear wheel puncture. The second Conquest in the background may have been super-imposed, although it could have been parked to act as a warning to traffic taking the hill at a run to avoid getting stuck in the snow. The date is also incorrect as no.23 left the Cheltenham fleet in March 1934! A 1931 Austin 7 is returning to its home in Winchcombe; despite its narrow tyres and light weight, it must have developed sufficient traction to climb the hill in these wintry conditions. (Ken Birkett collection)

Number 25 is seen in more detail in these two views. The 1932 Guy-bodied vehicle is seen outside the company's North Street office with a good load of passengers waiting to travel to Cleeve Hill. The vehicle is on this occasion decorated for the 1935 Silver Jubilee of King George V and Queen Mary. The large department store of E.L. Ward may be seen in the background on the corner of the High Street. Ward's was on the site until the late 1960s, when the site was purchased by Littlewood's. A few minutes later the vehicle moved off, and this nearside view was captured as it turned into Albion Street. Note the very solid looking Gas Co. offices on the street corner. An Austin 7 is following, having passed beneath the '25' bell, just a part of some obviously very lavish decorations.

Leckhampton departures on Service 3 for some years had their Centre terminus in the High Street, immediately before the Pittville Street junction. High Street traffic was of course two-way in those days; just a few years later, the prospect of buses waiting in this location would have been unthinkable as traffic volumes increased significantly. DG 9818 was the third vehicle to carry fleet no.1 and was seen late in 1936. It was numerically the first of the Weymann-bodied 1934 AEC Regents.

Looking immaculate on 23 May 1939 was no.2 (DG 9819); it was standing at the St Mark's shops terminus of service 4, which ran thence to Charlton Kings. Smartly attired conductor George Fitts stands by the radiator; he later became an ambulanceman in the town. In the background, in Shakespeare Road, a Martin Bros van goes about its business of delivering wines and spirits.

A splendid view of Cheltenham High Street in 1935. The gentleman with the walking stick in the foreground is standing on the corner of Regent Street. A motorcycle combination is passing Meesons, the chocolate manufacturers, while Sagar and Lawrence, jewellers, occupy the shop on the corner of Pittville Street. The whole scene is dominated by the bunting for the 1935 Silver Jubilee celebrations. The two buses in the centre of the view mark a significant advance in vehicle design over a five-year period. Emerging from Pittville Street is 1929 Invincible DF 8900, originally numbered 6 but by this time re-numbered 17. Loading for Leckhampton outside John Lance's premises is 1934 AEC Regent no.4 (DG 9821). A horse-drawn van and a hand-cart are making slow progress past Boot's the Chemist, behind the Regent.

The 1934 Regents displayed their route numbers at the rear; in this case no.3 (DG 9820) is on Service 2 to St Mark's and loads in Clarence Street outside the offices of surveyors Engall, Cox and Co. The bunting indicates that this was 1935. (Mike Rooum/PM Transport Photography)

In the standard post-war livery style, no.6 (DG 9823), numerically the final 1934 Regent, was laying over at the Cemetery terminus of Service 4 on 20 November 1948. The vehicle was then over fourteen years old, but still in fine condition. Just visible to the extreme left in the rear end view is one of the prefabs, then newly erected on the Prior's Farm estate.

Bradley Road terminus of Service 2 at Charlton Kings is the setting for this shot of no.5 (DG 9822) in the immediate post-war version of the Cheltenham livery. (W J Haynes)

The second batch of six Weymann-bodied AEC Regents arrived in 1936. They differed from the 1934 vehicles by having a separate front box for displaying the ultimate destination; these were however panelled over in the early post-war years. No. 7 (BAD 27) is seen here following that modification, and in the immediate post-war livery style. There had been an overnight snowfall when the vehicle was photographed at the LMS Station; the crew however still took the opportunity to get some (very) fresh air before taking up Service 4 to the Cemetery. Strangely, considering the weather, the two front upper deck windows appear to be open. (W J Haynes)

On the vehicles' next trip through the paint-shop they received this further revised livery, with very little cream. Number 8 (BAD 28) rests at the Bradley Road terminus in Charlton Kings; it was on Service 2. Bradley Road was for many years a cul-de-sac, but was eventually to provide access to Little Herberts Road. The terminus was in the form of a turning circle, alongside the main Cirencester Road, just a few hundred yards from the original Lilleybrook tram terminus. The vehicles were equipped with plentiful half-drop opening windows on both decks. (A D Packer)

Number 10 (BAD 30) is seen heading for Leckhampton on Service 3 on 23 May 1939. It is in the main shopping area of Bath Road, about to pass John Caudle's shoe shop and leather warehouse. The small lettering near the vehicle's rear corner states the vehicle's unladen weight as 6tons 19 cwt, and its speed limit as 30mph. Alongside the rear registration plate, the seating capacity is stated to be fifty-six.

Standing outside the LMS Station on 23 May 1939 was 1936 AEC Regent no.9 (BAD 29), heading for Lilleybrook. Another Weymann-bodied Regent is just visible in the background, heading for St Mark's.

The only known photograph of one of the later parcels vans, ADD 889, a 1935 Ford BF, displaying the later name of the Cheltenham District Traction Co. and the slogan: 'Send Your Parcels by our Express Transport Service'. (Frank Wood)

A few hundred yards back towards the town centre, but on the same day, no.12 (BAD 32) was also to be seen on Service 3. The destination display is fully utilised to show that the vehicle is travelling to Leckhampton via Pilley and that it will be calling at the College, Bath Road and the Norwood Arms. The vehicle was in fact outside the College when photographed. Most of the vehicle's windows are open, the good weather probably having attracted the photographer.

Four second-hand AEC Regents arrived in Cheltenham from Mansfield District late in 1938. They had been supplied new to that undertaking in 1934 and carried Weymann bodies. Very similar to the vehicles supplied new to Cheltenham, the main differences were in the simpler destination layouts and in the provision of fewer opening windows. VO 8585 became no.20 in the Cheltenham fleet. It is seen at St Mark's shops on 23 May 1939 driven by Bill Slatter.

Seen on the same day, sister vehicle VO 8588 (no.17) was working on Service 9. This service had been introduced only a short while before and ran from the town centre to the cemetery, serving the Whaddon Road area for the first time.

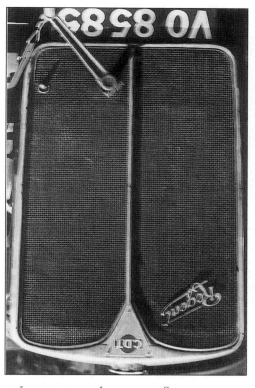

A standard option offered by AEC was to provide a customised radiator badge for the operators of their vehicles. Cheltenham District took up this option and most of its Regents carried badges in the AEC style but with CDT in place of the AEC initials. The detail is seen here on the radiator of VO 8585 (no.20).

When sixteen years old, VO 8586 (no.21) still looked very tidy when seen at Lansdown Station. The photographer was able to stand in the middle of the road to get this shot on 27 June 1950 – not something to be recommended in today's traffic conditions! At that time some Service 4 journeys still terminated at the station, by then officially known as the Midland Region station of British Railways.

More 1938 arrivals from Mansfield District were a trio of AEC Regal 4s, unusual four-cylinder vehicles, but with very attractive Weymann bodies. The vehicles dated from 1933; curiously, although they carried AAL registrations, they were older than the VO registered Regents. It seems that Mansfield had been allocated a large batch of VO numbers, which took some time to allocate as the Regents were delivered over a lengthy period. The three Cheltenham imports were AAL 108-110. These views of no.28 (AAL 109) were taken at the Cemetery terminus on 23 May 1939. The vehicle was on service 6 – note the route number in the rear box. The small oval plate on the lower rear panel confirms its PSV status in standard 1930s style, the licence number being 6017 in this case. The cut-away lower rear panel allowed for a spare wheel to be carried, but as the Cheltenham vehicles were never far from base, it was not necessary for one to be on board. Although fitted out to bus specification, these Regals were equipped with sliding roofs. Note too the emergency exit, comprising the centre rear panel, and the statement that the vehicle seated thirty-two passengers. A sign of the times was the display both inside and outside the vehicle of the National Service slogan – 'For the Protection of the Citizen'.

23 May 1939 proved to be a very successful day for Leslie Lapper's bus photography. Here at the junction of Arle Road and Brooklyn Road, the terminus of Service 8, he found 1938 Bedford WTB CDG 246, fleet number 19 – although this does not appear to be displayed. This was a unique vehicle in the Cheltenham fleet and it is suggested that it had been acquired for the Balfour Beatty group to compare its performance with the Dennis Aces which they had placed in service in Mansfield. The Bedford had a twenty-seat coach body by Duple, constructed in its Hendonian style with a straight waist rail. This vehicle was operated on a one-man basis by the driver, 'Pat' Teale, on this occasion. While most services ran across town, Service 8 ran only to the Centre. Its loadings were such that on Saturdays larger vehicles had to be provided.

Appendix I – Cheltenham And District Light Railway Company List Of Tramcars

Fleet No.	Year new	Builder	Type	Notes
1	1901	J Stephenson, New York	Open top double-deck	
2	1901	J Stephenson, New York	Open top double-deck	Briefly ran as single-deck
3	1901	J Stephenson, New York	Open top double-deck	Rebuilt to single deck
4	1901	J Stephenson, New York	Open top double-deck	
5	1901	J Stephenson, New York	Open top double-deck	
6	1901	J Stephenson, New York	Open top double-deck	
7	1901	J Stephenson, New York	Open top double-deck	
8	1901	J Stephenson, New York	Open top double-deck	
9	1902	Gloucester RCW	Single-deck	Rebuilt to open top double deck
10	1902	Gloucester RCW	Single-deck	
11	1902	Gloucester RCW	Open top double-deck	
12	1902	Gloucester RCW	Open top double-deck	Rebuilt to single deck
13	1905	British Thomson-Houston	Open top double-deck	
14	1905	British Thomson-Houston	Open top double-deck	Modernised, re-numbered 10
15	1905	British Thomson-Houston	Open top double-deck	
16	1905	British Thomson-Houston	Open top double-deck	Modernised
17	1905	British Thomson-Houston	Open top double-deck	
18	1905	British Thomson-Houston	Open top double-deck	
19	1905	British Thomson-Houston	Open top double-deck	Modernised, re-numbered 1
20	1905	British Thomson-Houston	Open top double-deck	
21	1921	English Electric	Open top double-deck	
22	1921	English Electric	Open top double-deck	
23	1921	English Electric	Open top double-deck	
24	(1921)	Birmingham & Midland	Open top double-deck	Ex-Worcester 1928
25	(1921)	Counties Joint Car Co	Open top double-deck	Ex-Worcester 1928

Appendix II – Cheltenham District Light Railway Company
Cheltenham District Traction Company
Listing Of Motor Buses Placed In Service Before 1939

Flt. No.	Reg. No.	Chassis	Chassis No.	Bodybuilder & no.	Seating	Date In	Date Out	Notes
none	?	Commer WP2	?	Commer.	B24F	-/13*	-/14	
?	DD 3956	Guy BB	1444	Strachan & Brown.	B30F	2/24*	-/32	
?	DD 3957	Guy BB	1443	Strachan & Brown.	B30F	2/24*	-/32	
3	DD 3955	Guy BB	1442	Strachan & Brown.	B30F	2/24*	4/32	
4	DD 8170	Guy BB	† 158/4	Strachan & Brown.	B28D	9/25*	8/32	
5	RA 4210	Guy B	C22431	Guy.	B26F	-/28	-/34	
6	DF 8900	Guy Invincible	FC23480	Guy.	027/24ROS	11/29*	8/38	17**
7	DF 8901	Guy Invincible	FC23481	Guy.	027/24ROS	11/29*	by-/44	RB. 18**
8	DF 8902	Guy invincible	FC23482	Guy.	027/24ROS	11/29*	by -/44	RB. 23**
9	DF 8903	Guy Invincible	FC23483	Guy.	027/24ROS	11/29*	12/35	
10	DF 8904	Guy Invincible	FC23484	Guy.	027/24ROS	11/29*	8/40	RB. 24**
11	DF 8905	Guy Invincible	FC23485	Guy.	027/24ROS	11/29* by 12/41		RB. 18**, 13**
12	DF 8906	Guy Invincible	FC23486	Guy.	027/24ROS	11/29* by 12/41		RB. 14**
13	DF 8907	Guy Invincible	FC23487	Guy.	027/24ROS	11/29*	5/37	
14	DF 8908	Guy Invincible	FC23488	Guy.	027/24ROS	11/29*	2/37	
15	DF 8909	Guy Invincible	FC23489	Guy.	027/24ROS	11/29*	c12/41	RB
16	PG 5606	Guy Invincible	FC23466	Hall Lewis.	027/27R	4/30	c/38	
17	DG 1310	Guy Conquest	C23677	Guy.	B28F	10/30*	3/34	
18	DG 1311	Guy Conquest	C23678	Guy.	B28F	10/30*	3/34	
19	DG 1312	Guy Conquest	C23679	Guy.	B28F	10/30*	3/34	
20	DG 1313	Guy Conquest	C23680	Guy.	B28F	10/30*	12/38	
21	DG 1314	Guy Conquest	C23681	Guy.	B28F	10/30*	12/38	
22	DG 1315	Guy Conquest	C23682	Guy.	B28F	10/30*	12/38	
23	DG 1316	Guy Conquest	C23683	Guy.	B28F	10/30*	3/34	
24	DG 1317	Guy Conquest	C23684	Guy.	B28F	10/30*	3/34	
25	DG 4474	Guy Invincible	FC23762	Guy.	B35TR	5/32*	-/39	
1	UE 9816	Guy OND	9424	Guy.	B20F	6/32	-/36	18**
2	UE 9319	Guy OND	9388	Guy.	B20F	6/32	-/38	19**
1	DG 9818	AEC Regent I	6612873	Weymann. M213	H30/24R	9/34*	1/49	
2	DG 9819	AEC Regent I	6612874	Weymann. M214	H30/24R	9/34*	9/47	
3	DG 9820	AEC Regent I	6612875	Weymann. M215	H30/24R	9/34*	10/47	
4	DG 9821	AEC Regent I	6612876	Weymann. M216	H30/24R	9/34*	1/49	
5	DG 9822	AEC Regent I	6612877	Weymann. M217	H30/24R	9/34*	6/50	
6	DG 9823	AEC Regent I	6612878	Weymann. M218	H30/24R	9/34*	12/49	
7	BAD 27	AEC Regent I	6613721	Weymann. M582	H30/26R	2/36*	6/50	
8	BAD 28	AEC Regent I	6613722	Weymann. M583	H30/26R	2/36*	6/50	
9	BAD 29	AEC Regent I	6613723	Weymann. M584	H30/26R	3/36*	9/50	
10	BAD 30	AEC Regent I	6613724	Weymann. M585	H30/26R	3/36*	10/47	
11	BAD 31	AEC Regent I	6613725	Weymann. M586	H30/26R	3/36*	-/44	
12	BAD 32	AEC Regent I	6613726	Weymann. M587	H30/26R	3/36*	12/48	
16	VO 8587	AEC Regent I	6612960	Weymann. M202	H28/26R	9/38	5/48	
17	VO 8588	AEC Regent I	6612961	Weymann. M203	H28/26R	9/38	-/39	

Flt. No.	Reg. No.	Chassis	Chassis No.	Bodybuilder & no.	Seating	Date In	Date Out	Notes
19	CDG 246	Bedford WTB	112165	Duple. 5006/2	C20F	4/38*	-/39	
20	VO 8585	AEC Regent I	6612958	Weymann. M200	H28/26R	11/38	3/51	
21	VO 8586	AEC Regent I	6612959	Weymann. M201	H28/26R	11/38	3/51	
26	AAL 110	AEC Regal 4	642054	Weymann. W961	B32F	2/39	-/40	
27	AAL 108	AEC Regal 4	642052	Weymann. W959	B32F	11/38	-/40	
28	AAL 109	AEC Regal 4	642053	Weymann. W960	B32F	2/39	-/40	

Notes

Although chassis numbers are mandatory, only certain body-builders allocated body numbers.

†   The chassis number quoted for DD 8170 is in fact thought to be its Guy sales number

*   Indicates that the vehicle was supplied new to the Company on the date shown; all other vehicles were acquired second-hand; details of their former owners appear in the body of the text.

**   Indicates that the vehicle was renumbered, and what the new number was.

RB   Indicates that the vehicle was later fitted with a replacement body; full details of all such rebuilds and other modifications appear within the main body of this book.

Vehicles On Loan To The Company Before 1939

Reg. No.	Chassis	Bodybuilder	Seating	Date in	Date out	Hired from
BM 26x0	Commer WP	Commer	Ch14	-/13	-/13	Commer Cars
RA 3958	Tilling-Stevens B10B	Strachan & Brown	B32F	2/28	by 1/29	Midland General
RA 3959	Tilling-Stevens B10B	Strachan & Brown	B32F	2/28	by 1/29	Midland General

Note: the third digit of the Commer registration number is not known

Ancillary Motor Vehicles In Use Before 1939

Reg.No	Chassis	Type	Date In	Date Out
AD 525	Thomas 40hp	car	6/05	?
AD 2700	Renault 9hp	van	9/12	?
AD 2767	Renault 10hp	van	12/12	1/21
DD 5530	FWD	tower wagon	10/24	12/31
?	Arrol Johnson	car (later van)	?	?
DD 8226	Morris T	van	10/25	?
DG 991	Ford AA	van	8/30	?
AAD 669	Ford Y	van	1/35	?
ADD 889	Ford BF	van	3/35	?
BDG 315	Ford Y	van	12/36	?
DDD 820	Ford Y	van	12/38	?